HITTING THE LOTTERY JACKPOT

STATE GOVERNMENTS AND THE TAXING OF DREAMS

DAVID NIBERT

Monthly Review Press

New York

To Julie and Taylor

Library of Congress Cataloging-in-Publication Data
Nibert, David Alan, 1953–
    Hitting the lottery jackpot : government and the taxing of dreams
/ David Nibert.
        p.   cm.
    Includes bibliographical references and index.
    ISBN 1–58367–014–9 (pbk.)—ISBN 1–58367–013–3 (cloth)
    1. Lotteries—United States.   2. Lotteries—United States—States.
3. Gambling—United States.   4. Revenue—United States.
5. Lotteries—Government policy—United States.   6. n-us.
I. Title.
HG6126.N53   2000   99–27818
336.1'7'0973–dc21   CIP

ISBN 1–58367–014–9 (paper)
ISBN 1–58367–013–3 (cloth)

Monthly Review Press
122 West 27th Street
New York, NY 10001

Designed and typeset by Lucy Morton & Robin Gable, Grosmont
Manufactured in Canada by Transcontinental
10   9   8   7   6   5   4   3   2   1

CONTENTS

ACKNOWLEDGMENTS

I would like to thank Julie Ford, my spouse, whose comments and editorial skills were invaluable in the development of this work. Thanks also to Steve Rumbaugh for his technical assistance in creating figures and charts used in early drafts of the manuscript. Finally, thanks to the staff and associates of Monthly Review Press for their encouragement, support, and expertise.

ONE

THE RISE OF LOTTOMANIA

In a relatively short period of time, national and state lotteries have become not only part of our society, but part of our day-to-day experience. Advertisements for the lotteries feed people's desire for change: "All you need is a dollar and a dream." Newspapers, magazines, and television widely publicize the life-altering consequences of winning the lottery, and parade winners before the public. But the harm caused by lotteries to individuals is rarely noticed or publicized.

In the United States, Richard Smith, a nineteen-year-old Pennsylvania man, spent his savings buying six thousand one-dollar lottery tickets in his efforts to win a $2.5 million jackpot. After failing to win, he attempted suicide. Then there is the case of Richard Clary, a forty-one-year-old Florida business executive, who was charged with grand theft after embezzling $500,000 to support a $5,000-a-week lottery habit. And Tom and Philomena Drake of Harrisburg, Pennsylvania, who spent their $14,000 savings trying to win the state lottery. There are accounts of a middle-aged homemaker in Delaware who spent thousands in vain trying to hit the lottery, and a bank teller in Toronto who embezzled $80,000 in an unsuccessful attempt to win a million-dollar jackpot.[1] Motivated by a $295.7 million lottery jackpot, a Bronx waiter spent his entire trade-school tuition, $3,000, on Powerball tickets.[2]

In the U.K., lottery obsession and disappointment have produced fatal consequences. For instance, Timothy O'Brien, a fifty-one-year-old tool inspector and father of two, routinely purchased a weekly batch of tickets he shared with a friend. In April 1995, O'Brien forgot to make the weekly purchase; after the draw he wrongly thought that the numbers he and his friend had selected were the six winning numbers. (In fact, they had picked only four.) After writing a note to his friend apologizing for not making the purchase, O'Brien killed himself in the attic of his Liverpool home.[3] Also in the U.K., Joy Senior, a twenty-eight-year-old mother of three described as happy and loving, became convinced her psychic boyfriend would win the lottery. When he lost, Senior became despondent, convinced she had somehow ruined his psychic powers. Senior stabbed her three young children to death before drowning herself.[4] Lamenting the social impact of the U.K. National Lottery, the Right Reverend Nigel McCulloch commented, "There is … the serious issue of the raising of false hopes. It was said the lottery would be harmless entertainment but it cannot be when you present people with the possibility of winning so much."[5]

In the United States lotteries have been in existence since before many of today's young people were born, and lotteries seem a normal part of daily life and state finance. But what is the history of lotteries in the United States? Why were they banned at the end of the nineteenth century? What conditions prompted states to reestablish lotteries? Why does a large portion of the public support state lotteries? Are state lotteries a fair and ethical method of raising revenues? Do they really benefit schools? How do lotteries bolster citizens' loyalty to a society characterized by profound disparities in the distribution of wealth and income?

The Rebirth of State Lotteries

On April 22, 1964, officers of the Rhode Island state police followed Louis Hamod as he approached the state line. When he crossed into Massachusetts they pulled over and waited. Five hours later the police spotted Hamod returning. When he crossed back into the state his car was halted and Hamod, a sixty-three-year-old Rhode Island restaurant owner, was arrested for the possession of illegal materials—New Hampshire lottery tickets.

Little more than a month earlier, the governor of New Hampshire, John W. King, had orchestrated an event to attract people like Louis Hamod to the state. On March 13, 1964, Governor King bought the first state lottery ticket to be sold in the United States since the end of the nineteenth century, when lotteries—contests in which participants can win prizes based entirely on chance—were made illegal. At the time, federal law prohibited interstate trafficking in lottery-related materials, and many state constitutions prohibited the operation of lotteries. So when state lottery tickets first went on sale in New Hampshire on Friday the 13th, the *Portsmouth Herald* reported that "an air of uneasiness prevailed among the ticket purchasers."[6] But after the governor purchased a ticket, followed by a member of the New Hampshire legislature, sales were brisk. In mid-July 1964, New Hampshire lottery officials, still concerned with the respectability of the enterprise, strove to legitimize the activity by flanking themselves with local beauty queens and a band playing "The Star Spangled Banner" as they selected lottery finalists.

A great deal of debate had preceded the creation of the lottery in New Hampshire. After intense public hearings in the New Hampshire legislature, the House and Senate approved the measure that Governor King signed into law on April 30, 1963. Lottery proponents maintained that the lottery, which they called the "sweepstakes," would create sorely needed funds for the state's education system. Having no state income tax or sales tax, New Hampshire's funding for education was the lowest in the nation.

However, lottery critics bristled at the legislation, challenging the morality of what some referred to as a "sin tax." The Episcopal Bishop of New Hampshire, the Reverend Charles F. Hall, denounced the new lottery as "a cheap expedient that would tarnish New Hampshire's historical reputation for courageous and forthright political leadership" and a "miserable intruder" upon the interests of the state and nation. The state's Superintendent of Schools, Harlan E. Atherton, called for sounder methods of raising state funds and stated: "I am quite liberal in many respects but I take a dim view of government by wager and subjecting education to the vagaries of volunteer contributions."[7] Concord, New Hampshire, Mayor Charles Campbell Davies called the creation of the state lottery "The damnedest thing that ever happened in the history of the state: a black day for New Hampshire."[8]

Criticism of the policy came from outside the state as well. Senator Everett Dirksen of Illinois publicly denounced New Hampshire's lottery, believing "it corrupts the morals of people."[9] And the ranking bishop of the Methodist Church in the United States, Bishop John Wesley Lord, wired Governor King that he considered the day the law was signed a "black Tuesday."[10]

The moral indignation that the creation of the New Hampshire state lottery prompted was accompanied by questions about its legality, and it was these questions that led the Rhode Island state police to follow and arrest Louis Hamod. Realizing the population of New Hampshire was not large enough to sustain a profitable state lottery,

lottery promoters there hoped it would also find customers among tourists and residents of nearby states. However, federal law prohibited the transportation of lottery tickets or materials across state lines, the Federal Communications Commission prohibited radio and television broadcast of any lottery information, the U.S. Postal Service prohibited the sending of any lottery information through the mail, and state law in neighboring Rhode Island, New Jersey, and Massachusetts made it illegal even to possess a lottery ticket.

Nonetheless, law enforcement officials realized that, despite strong repudiation of the lottery in some sectors of society, the public strongly supported it. Governor King's mail favored the lottery ten to one and, in a referendum prompted by lottery opponents in New Hampshire, 80 percent of voters supported the lottery. Lottery proponents also argued it would be unfair to enforce laws that suppressed lotteries when promotion and participation in the Irish Sweepstakes had been overlooked for years. When Louis Hamod appeared in court the judge said the state police's action was "akin to entrapment"; he granted defense motions to suppress the seized evidence, and the charges were dropped. On the federal level, United States Attorney Raymond J. Pettine announced that Justice Department policy toward interstate trafficking in lottery materials, particularly the possession of lottery tickets, would be to "decline Federal prosecution when a reputable citizen is involved."[11] Pettine said the Justice Department would act only in a case in which commercial exploitation of the lottery as a gambling business was attempted. Moral and legal issues were not the only obstacles to New Hampshire's efforts to establish a state lottery. The Internal Revenue Service (IRS) also created problems for lottery proponents. When New Hampshire was planning its lottery in 1963, the IRS stated its intention to tax lottery revenues. However, because state revenues from betting on horse races were not taxed, New Hampshire officials created the lottery in such a way that the ultimate winner was determined by a yearly horse race—thus averting federal taxation of lottery profits.

Following New Hampshire's success in creating and defending the lottery, several members of the New York Legislature urged the creation of a lottery in that state. A lottery, they argued, would help to fund the needs of cities and provide for school construction and hospitals. Predictably, a campaign against a New York lottery was begun. The state Council of Churches called such wagering a "social and moral sin" and declared: "Attaching an evil habit to a good and needy cause does nothing for the cause and only feeds the habit."[12] New York Governor Nelson Rockefeller joined the Board of Regents of the state public education system in denouncing the lottery proposal. The Board of Regents declared: "We believe that attempts to support public education by the lottery involve serious moral considerations and, in our opinion, are inconsistent with the goals of education."[13] However, in November 1966, 61 percent of the voters supported the lottery proposal, and the New York lottery was in operation by 1969.[14]

As in New Hampshire, the New York lottery was tied to a horse race to avoid federal taxation. Although the annual horse races were exciting, the months of waiting to find out if one was a winner dampened the enthusiasm of many potential lottery players. Following the initial excitement during the first year of lottery operation, ticket sales in both states declined steadily for the next five years.

Lottery proponents in New Jersey learned from the experience of their neighbors. After 89 percent of New Jersey voters supported the creation of a lottery, its lottery began in 1971. New Jersey lottery officials sought to generate greater player enthusiasm through more frequent drawings. While New Hampshire and New York lottery tickets were priced at one dollar each, New Jersey officials set the ticket price at only fifty cents. Instead of linking the drawings to future horse races, the New Jersey lottery based the selection of winners on the results of past horse races that were randomly selected. New Jersey held drawings weekly, and then daily. And while New Hampshire limited ticket sale locations to state liquor stores and horse tracks, New Jersey was much more flexible, soon establishing more than three thousand lottery ticket vendors. Tickets could be purchased at grocery stores, gasoline stations, news stands, taverns, restaurants, department stores, and pharmacies. New Jersey Lottery drawings were highly publicized media events modeled after television game shows of the day.

Unlike New Hampshire and New York, where lottery tickets did not sell in the numbers projected, New Jersey ticket sales far exceeded expectations. New York soon followed New Jersey's example, boosting ticket sales by lowering ticket prices to fifty cents and by instituting weekly drawings. New Jersey's success also spurred lottery proponents in other states. During the 1970s lotteries were created in ten more states and, despite repeated expressions of concern about the immorality of gambling and the unfairness of such a method of public financing, by 1998 lotteries were providing revenues for thirty-seven states and the District of Columbia.[15]

Although lotteries have been resisted in the South, that resistance has eroded as lawmakers in Alabama, North Carolina, South Carolina, and Tennessee have seen their residents spend tens of millions of dollars on the neighboring Georgia lottery. In 1998, gubernatorial candidates in Alabama and South Carolina campaigned on the promise of a new state lottery, and each was elected—defeating an anti-lottery opponent in each case. In the spring of 1999, the Alabama legislature authorized a voter referendum on the proposed lottery in the autumn of 1999, and the South Carolina legislature authorized a similar ballot issue for the year 2000. Similar legislative efforts are under way in North Carolina and Tennessee.

Although legalized lotteries are a relatively recent development in the modern United States, they are not new to many other countries. One hundred and forty nations throughout the world permit some form of legalized gambling, and lotteries are legal in more than one hundred.[16] Countries as diverse as Nigeria, France, Mexico, and the Philippines all have national lotteries. Lotteries, and all other forms of gambling, have been prohibited in Islamic countries; however, there is evidence that the lure of the lottery is being felt there as well. For example, although gambling is illegal under Indonesian and Islamic law, the government there has euphemistically called its state-sponsored lottery "Philanthropic Donations with Prizes."[17]

One of the countries that instituted a lottery most recently was the United Kingdom. After a ban of roughly 168 years, a national lottery was reestablished in the U.K. in 1994, sparked in no small part by the proliferation of lotteries in other Western European nations. As in the United States, many were opposed to the creation of the lottery, especially the clergy. In response to an early 1994 jackpot of £17.8 million, the Right Reverend Nigel McCulloch, the Bishop of Wakefield, lamented the fact that such a sum was going to a single winner. "I think of what £18 million could do for some still-deprived people in some areas here in West Yorkshire.... We have got 80 percent unemployment and £18 million would be able to do a lot for entire communities."[18]

The Evolution of Lottery Games

The type of game first used by the New Hampshire and New York lotteries, the "sweepstakes," is referred to as a "passive game" because participants purchase a ticket with a preprinted number on it and have nothing to do but wait for a drawing, sometimes months away. While the weekly drawings in New Jersey's lottery helped to generate greater enthusiasm, the essentially passive nature of the game remained a problem. Knowing that some form of purchaser participation would generate more interest and sales, a business that sold lottery-related products to states, Scientific Games, Inc., developed an instant game. First offered in New Jersey and Massachusetts, the instant game permitted ticket buyers to participate by scratching an opaque, latex-coated ticket to reveal whether they had won. The purchaser, now the "player," had an active, although simple, role in the process. The successful elements of the developing formula for instant lottery games were player participation, a degree of suspense generated by scratching a ticket, and the immediacy of learning whether one is a winner. Unlike the earlier passive drawings, instant games offered far smaller prizes, with a much higher percentage of players winning from one to one hundred dollars. The concept was so successful that by 1982 all state lotteries were operating some form of instant game.[19]

As the states celebrated the relative success of their lotteries, they remained envious of the money still going into the illegal numbers games that had thrived for decades before the legalization of lotteries. In the illegal games, players selected their own numbers, a factor that dramatically increased interest and participation in the game because some players believe that selection of a winning number is based on some form of skill. This provided the player with an illusory sense of control, even though, barring some sort of fraud, the winning numbers for the illegal games were generated in conjunction with daily horse races and essentially were randomly determined. Since there is no skill that can help one guess a randomly selected number, the sense of control fostered by these games is indeed a false one. Nonetheless, the illegal numbers games, which commonly involved players trying to predict a three- or four-digit number in exact order or three numbers in any order, flourished.

The potential market for such a game, where the illusion of control was so enticing to players, was too much to resist for state lottery officials who were striving to increase lottery sales and revenues. The states appropriated the numbers games with little change, developing daily numbers games that generally paid prizes much larger than the instant games but substantially less than the sweepstakes jackpots.

Next came the game that is now most closely associated with state lotteries, Lotto. First introduced in New Jersey in 1978, Lotto combines elements of the old sweepstakes drawing used by New Hampshire in the 1960s with the enticing features of the illicit numbers games. In Lotto, players pick their own numbers from a specified field, usually picking between five and seven numbers. For example, in a 6/45 format, players select six numbers between one and forty-five. Unlike the daily numbers games, the odds against successfully picking the six numbers are astronomical, but so are the prizes. If no one selects the right numbers, picked during weekly drawings, the jackpot accumulates, sometimes reaching tens of millions of dollars.

"Do you want to stop and buy a lottery ticket?" I recently overheard a husband ask his wife in a coffee shop. "Why?" she replied, "The jackpot is *only* four million." This exchange reflects a basic tenet of lottery participation: the bigger the jackpot, the greater the excitement and the more people play. For example, in June of 1994, when New Jersey's Lotto jackpot climbed to $38.9 million, more than 21.9 million tickets were purchased.[20] "Everybody's acting crazy," declared Elaine Gibson of Gus's Grocery and Carryout in Moraine, Ohio, when the Ohio Superlotto jackpot reached $40 million in March, 1995. "Individuals are playing 10 and 20 times more than they normally do."[21]

The excitement created by enormous jackpots is not confined to the United States. When the U.K. National Lottery jackpot climbed to £35 million in January 1996 "sales were running at about 40 per cent above a normal week," and hourly sales records were surpassed easily.[22]

Recognizing that large jackpots generate ticket sales, a number of smaller states that are unable to generate a large jackpot individually have cooperated in the creation of a multi-state lottery called Powerball. Powerball players try to match five numbers, plus a Powerball number. Twenty states and the District of Columbia jointly sponsor the multi-state Lotto, increasing lottery revenues in each state. Tickets are sold by vendors in each state, and the jackpots can be enormous: in March 1995, a fifty-five-year-old secretary from Phoenix won $101.8 million. The largest Lotto jackpot to date was $295.7 million, shared by thirteen machine-shop workers in Ohio.

Who Profits from Lotteries?

The dramatic growth of state lotteries can be seen in gross sales over the years. In 1973, state lotteries sold more than $600 million in tickets.[23] Fifteen years later, combined sales for lottery tickets across the country had climbed to approximately $16 billion.[24] In 1993, $25.3

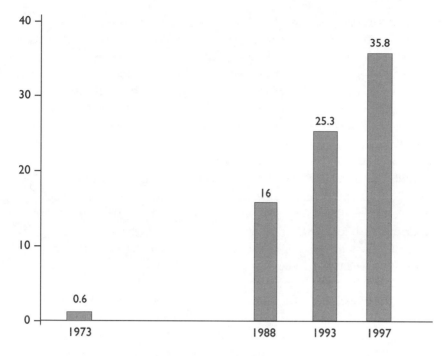

Figure 1.1   U.S. state lottery sales (billion), selected years

billion per year was spent in the United States on lottery games.[25] By 1997, lottery sales ballooned to $35.8 billion (see Figure 1.1).[26]

State lotteries have become big business. In a *Forbes* magazine survey in 1990, state lotteries jointly ranked twenty-fourth in gross sales among U.S. businesses, just below United Technologies.[27] And state governments are not the only ones cashing in on the enormous sums generated by state lotteries. Lotteries have been a boon to businesses that manufacture lottery-related equipment and products, such as Syntech International, Scientific Games, Inc., Webcraft Games, GTECH, and Control Data Corporation, all of which make millions of dollars every year from contracts with states to provide everything from on-line computer services to instant games. GTECH, one of the largest suppliers of lottery equipment in the business, produces computer and communication systems for lotteries. The Rhode Island company implemented the first on-line Lotto in 1978 and saw sales grow during the 1980s from $33 million to $126 million.[28]

State lotteries have also been very good to ticket vendors, the stores, service stations, taverns, restaurants, and other businesses that operate lottery computer terminals and sell the tickets. On average, the lottery ticket vendors take in a 5.5 percent commission on all their sales and, in many states, a vendor who sells a winning Lotto ticket also receives a small percentage of the jackpot. It is not surprising, then, that vendors heavily advertise the fact that they have lottery tickets and games for sale, accounting for the proliferation of state lottery signs that now litter both urban and rural landscapes.

Still, the promotion by the ticket vendors is greatly eclipsed by the work of the advertising agencies hired by the states to continually dream up new ways to get the public to buy lottery tickets. The dramatic and continued increase in the sale of lottery tickets is due in no small part to the ads and commercials that reach us through our car radios, magazines and newspapers and that enter our homes via the Internet and also our televisions in the form of commercials, televised drawings, and lottery-based game shows.

The advertising industry has profited very nicely from the creation of state lotteries. In 1990, state lotteries in the United States spent $294 million on lottery advertising.[29] It is the advertising agencies that bear the primary responsibility for maintaining and expanding lottery ticket sales. They are constantly creating new instant scratch-off games, modeled on poker, baseball, bingo, and a wide variety of other themes designed to keep instant game players from losing interest. The director of the Oregon state lottery, James Davey, explains:

> We have gambling themes, we do Olympics. At Christmas we do Holiday Cash. With Lucky Stars we play on people's astrological signs. We find that if you run two or three, four or five games at the same time, you'll sell more tickets. People say, "I'm not lucky at Lucky Stars, but I'm sure good at basketball."[30]

Advertising agencies were primarily responsible for the creation of lottery television game shows. Ohio, the first state to start a lottery game show, broadcast its four hundredth lottery show program in September 1994, claiming to have entertained more than three thousand contestants while giving away more than $47 million.[31] Ohio's *Cash Explosion* program, introduced in 1987, followed the television game show formula of a panel of contestants competing for cash prizes. Like the other lottery games, and unlike other TV game shows, however, skill plays no role in the televised lottery game. Players simply select squares on a game board searching for randomly placed prizes.

Viewer interest is generated by vicarious suspense as the contestants search the game board for cash and prizes. The activity is dressed up by flashing lights and sound effects on the game board and by chirpy, smiling hosts. An enthusiastic studio audience is attracted by the chance to win door prizes from $100 to $1,000.

A big incentive for viewers to tune in to the lottery shows every week is the on-the-air drawing for the next week's contestants. To become a contestant, a lottery player must purchase a specific instant game, such as Ohio's *Cash Explosion* or Illinois's *Fortune Hunt*. When scratched, some of the instant game tickets will reveal that they are "entry tickets"; holders of entry tickets who mail them to the state lottery commission are included in a random drawing for participation in the televised program. Other incentives for people to watch the program are variations of "at-home play." For example, the Illinois program *Fortune Hunt* has a segment called "at-home bonus play," where holders of instant game tickets have a chance to win a cash prize if a number on their ticket is randomly selected during the program.

Constant variations on instant games, televised lottery game shows, and perpetual advertising campaigns have contributed to the growth of state lotteries, and new strategies are always being developed to expand lottery participation and sales. For example, a number of states have developed lottery ticket vending machines, making the purchase of lottery tickets impersonal and anonymous. Another new strategy is the introduction of video lottery machines. Much like variations of video poker, these machines are essentially self-serve vending terminals equipped with seductive lights and sounds. However, like the scratch-off tickets, player skill has little to do with winning, as opportunities to win are preprogrammed. Five states—Delaware, Oregon, Rhode Island, South Dakota and West Virginia—are using the video lottery machines. Most states have resisted video lottery due to its strong resemblance to slot machines, which are illegal in most states. However, the push for video lottery has not subsided. For example, in Ohio the vending machine industry and the hospitality industry (bars and taverns) have created the Ohio Video·Lottery Coalition, which is lobbying state government to approve video lottery in Ohio. Coalition spokesperson Dick George, president of Roy George Music and Vending, pitches the concept this way:

> Our blue collar customer who is traditionally stopping in his neighborhood gin mill at the end of the day to spend a few bucks and relax with his friends may stop once a week now ... and the other days he'll pick up a video and maybe

a six-pack and go home. Not only does the hospitality industry lose that patron, but the coin machine industry does as well. In other words, we need traffic ... we need warm bodies to be successful in our operations.[32]

So far, the Ohio legislature has resisted the video lottery coalition's efforts.

Another innovative direction in lottery marketing has been the development of sports-related lottery games. In 1989, Oregon instituted a "Sports Action" lottery game that linked lottery play with professional basketball and football. In the 1980s the University of Oregon lagged far behind other Pacific-10 Conference schools in the funding of intercollegiate athletics and faced a $3 million program deficit. Voters had rejected a 1988 referendum proposing a sales tax increase on beer and cigarettes to finance the athletics programs. Promoters of the new lottery game claimed it was the only practical way to fund intercollegiate athletics in Oregon. The Sports Action game permits players to fill out parley cards in which they bet on the winners, based on point spreads, of a specified number of games, with bets ranging from $1 to $20 per card. Winners must be picked in each game for a player to collect.

The National Football League criticized the new lottery game, claiming that it constituted "a genuine threat to the integrity of our sport" that in the long run could "break down public confidence in the game."[33] Despite its threat of legal action, the N.F.L. did not try to stop the new lottery game from going into effect. However, the National Basketball Association did file suit against the Oregon lottery; in a settlement the state agreed not to include the N.B.A. in any lottery games for five years. By January 1994 the Oregon Lottery Sports Action game had earned $9.8 million for the state's Intercollegiate Athletic and Scholarship Fund.[34]

The purchase of lottery tickets is now riding the wave of increasingly sophisticated communications technology in the home. States now have lottery websites. Individuals can buy lottery tickets over the Internet, charging their ticket purchases to credit cards. The development of interactive television may well also facilitate the continued expansion of state lottery play.

Lottery Culture

The extension of lottery culture into our everyday lives can be seen in numerous books and movies. Take, for example, the 1994 film *It Could Happen to You*, with Nicolas Cage and Bridget Fonda as a police officer and a waitress who split a lottery prize. The film both reflects and perpetuates the fantasy of having your life suddenly changed by winning millions of dollars. This fantasy is also the theme of Judith Michael's *Pot of Gold*. The following passage from this novel allows the reader to enjoy vicariously the spending spree of lottery winner Claire Goddard, a woman previously of "modest means," and her daughter Emma.

> The car was a white Mercedes with white leather upholstery. Emma said it looked like an ambulance. "Well, pick another color, then." Claire said. And when Emma put an admiring hand on the hood of a cherry red, two-seat Mercedes sports car with black leather upholstery, Claire nodded casually to the salesman. "We'll take that one, too." Emma gasped. "Two cars?" "I thought you might like to have one at college." "I might like—? Oh, Mother!" Emma threw her arms around Claire. "You're incredible. Everything's incredible. Isn't everything totally off-the-wall incredible?"[35]

In the next passage, Claire walks through her new house purchased for $1.25 million.

> All the delivery men were gone, but still Claire roamed through the rooms of the house. This is mine, she told herself, this is mine, this is mine. She loved the brilliant reds and blacks and blues of the Oriental rugs against the shining floors; she loved the red couches and soft taupe armchairs and curtain-less windows that looked out into the gardens; she loved the dark green walls of the library with its white couches and walnut shelves, empty now but, by tomorrow, she thought, with the three of them working, filled with all their books. She loved ... the silence of her bedroom, a spacious high-ceilinged room with a fireplace at one end, furnished in apricot and white, with lace curtains at the high windows. My room, she thought, my home. I cannot believe all this is mine.[36]

Television and newspapers spread stories of the splendors of lottery wealth to would-be winners. Take the case of David N. Demarest, for example. In 1992 Mr. Demarest was fifty-two years old, bankrupt and sharing with his twenty-one-year-old son a cramped one-bedroom apartment overlooking the New Jersey Turnpike. Mr. Demarest had installed telephones for New Jersey Bell for almost twenty-five years. Then, like millions of others seeking to improve their lives through the remote chance of winning—in Mr. Demarest's case a one in 9.3 million chance—he bought a ticket for the New Jersey lottery. Mr. Demarest found himself holding one of the four winning tickets for a record $44.3 million jackpot; his share of the winnings was $440,000 a year for twenty years, after taxes. According to the *New York Times*:

His life had changed in more happy ways than even he anticipated.... Now, more than eight years after getting divorced, he and his ex-wife, Margaret, are living together.... His son, Scott, a warehouse worker who inherited the Wood-bridge apartment after Mr. Demarest paid off the mortgage, seized his new-found security and was married.... His daughter, Midge, who had been working at a gas station, decided to go to college.[37]

Mr. Demarest and his ex-wife bought an oceanfront home in a coastal town near Cape Canaveral, Florida.

He is still humbled by the house. Set back from the road on a professionally landscaped lot where the grass is bordered by palms and other tropical plants, it is in stark contrast with some of the shed-sized homes down the road from him. His bedroom encompasses the entire second floor, 58 feet by 30 feet.... From his backyard, with its panoramic view of the ocean, he can almost believe this is paradise.[38]

Television and newspaper advertisements also entice people to dream of wealth by dangling extravagant homes and cars before their eyes. In some instances advertisers even use fantasy to induce fantasy. For example, in March 1994 the New York lottery lured players with an image of a stately mansion with luxurious gardens and ornate interiors. The estate, however, did not exist. The ad was a compilation that included the Vanderbilt Mansion in Hyde Park, New York, a famous seventeenth-century garden at Sceaux in France, and interiors from the seventy-nine-room Mills Mansion in Staatsburg, New York. The composite was further "computer-enhanced" before being presented to the public with the slogan "All you need is a dollar and a dream."[39]

A Sociological View of Lotteries

The objections and concerns expressed by the lottery detractors are fast becoming mere historical footnotes. However, do the concerns about fairness, justice, and thoughtful social policy have any basis? This book will use a sociological vantage point to examine the rebirth, proliferation, and consequences of state lotteries. The specific socio-logical perspective that will be used here to examine state lotteries is the conflict perspective, particularly as it has been influenced by Marx-ian theory.

One of the most enduring legacies of Karl Marx is his illumination of the powerful role that economic forces exert on social arrange-ments. How people produce and distribute goods and resources strongly affects how they organize their society, and how they relate to one another, as well the ideas they shape about what constitutes acceptable behavior. Marx noted that, for the past ten thousand years, powerful ruling elites have exerted profound influence over economic arrangements—arrangements structured to their substantial advantage. Moreover, these elites utilized other social forces, such as the political, religious, and educational systems in their societies, to legitimate and protect unequal and oppressive economic arrangements. Most people, both in the past and the present, largely have accepted these arrangements because they have been taught to believe in the ideas that support the status quo. In general, these ideas exalt the privileged while devaluing those with few resources. As we will see, the Marxian perspective will help to illuminate both the recent reemergence of lotteries and the political-economic conditions that facilitated their growth.

In the next chapter we will see that lotteries were created and used as capitalism emerged from late feudal society, even though the games were widely viewed at the time as "unjust and fraudulent." Lotteries were used to fund colonial expansion and public works in the Western Hemisphere, despite persistent disapproval from numerous religious quarters. Notwithstanding long-term efforts to abolish lotteries during the eighteenth and nineteenth centuries on moral grounds, the demise of lotteries in the U.S. in the late nineteenth century resulted primarily from the development of institutionalized forms of capital creation consistent with the growth of capitalism—that is, moral arguments prevailed only after lotteries were no longer necessary, revenue-creating devices. The second portion of the chapter examines the development of corporate capitalism in the twentieth-century United States and the resulting dependence of the average person on decisions made by the few who control huge corporations. It is suggested that the drive for profit facilitated late-twentieth-century deindustrialization, disinvestment at home, and investments in "business-friendly" nations abroad. These forces led to reduced quality of life for countless people now dependent on the corporate-controlled economy and reduced the tax funds that once flowed into state coffers. Thus, economic necessity led to the reemergence of state lotteries, and individual economic distress and uncertainty fostered public demand for the perceived economic opportunity that lotteries offered.

Chapter 3 indicts state governments for promoting a public policy that is patently unfair to people with few resources because a lottery is a regressive form of taxation. Nonetheless, states exhort their citizens to buy lottery tickets through a never-ending campaign of glossy ads and television commercials. Targeting such groups as African Americans for special promotions, state governments use deceptive campaigns that mislead the public about their chances of winning as well as about the way lottery funds are used. Evidence is presented to suggest that state governments are contributing to increased gambling in all forms as well as to the prevalence of compulsive gambling. The second portion of the chapter maintains that such irresponsible public policy is not an aberration; rather, this government effort actually is consistent with the true nature of the state in capitalist society. As evidence, the ways the state has facilitated the growth and interests of the wealthy through favorable laws and policies over the past thirty years—actions that led to the creation of contemporary state lotteries—are briefly reviewed.

Chapter 4 begins with a brief review of the ways in which social inequalities are legitimated in the United States. Noting that people in the U.S. have been indoctrinated to believe that opportunities for wealth are available to anyone who works hard, it is maintained that state lotteries buttress this belief in opportunity for individual economic advancement. Moreover, state promotion of lotteries frequently conveys the message that the acquisition of wealth is a wonderful, transcendent experience available to all, thus legitimating the existence of both great wealth and poverty. Lotteries also tend to serve as a safety valve, providing those in economic distress with illusory goals while diverting their attention from the economic and political forces that are primarily responsible for their fate. Finally, it is maintained that state governments even stoop to promoting public belief in magic and supernatural forces by exhorting people to bet their "lucky numbers" and facilitating the widespread growth of psychic consultants who profit from the "services" provided to economically disenfranchised people. Finally, Chapter 5 suggests that the problems that facilitated the reemergence of lotteries in the 1970s and 1980s continued into the 1990s. It considers what people with low and moderate incomes can do to stem the growth of lotteries in the twenty-first century and to promote social justice.

First, however, this examination of lotteries will begin with history. Like classical sociological writers such as Marx, sociologists today use history to illuminate the patterns of daily life. As the eminent twentieth-century sociologist C. Wright Mills wrote:

> No social study that does not come back to the problems of biography, of history, and of their intersections within a society has completed its intellectual journey.[40]

This analysis will begin, then, with a brief examination of the history of lotteries in the United States and the factors that have contributed to their revival in the late twentieth century.

Notes

1. H. Roy Kaplan, "The Social and Economic Impact of State Lotteries," *The Annals of the American Academy of Political and Social Science*, July 1984, 103.
2. Clyde Haberman, "The Specter of Instant Wealth," *New York Times*, July 31, 1998, B1.
3. Nigel Bunyan, "Father Shot Himself Over Jackpot That Never Was," *Electronic Telegraph*, June 16, 1995, 1, http://www.telegraph.co.uk.
4. Wendy Holden, "Mother Who Killed Her Three Children Was Depressed Over Lottery," *Electronic Telegraph*, September 7, 1995, 1, www.telegraph. co.uk.
5. Hugh Muir, *Electronic Telegraph*, 1.
6. *Portsmouth Herald*, March 13, 1964, 1.
7. *New York Times Magazine*, May 19, 1963, 104.
8. Ibid., 16.
9. *New York Times*, May 2, 1963, 35: 2.
10. Ibid.
11. *New York Times*, March 28, 1964, 8: 8.
12. *New York Times*, January 16, 1964, 46: 4.
13. Charles T. Clotfelter and Philip J. Cook, *Selling Hope: State Lotteries in America* (Cambridge, MA: Harvard University Press, 1989), 144.
14. Ibid.
15. North American Association of State and Provincial Lotteries, *Lottery Facts and Background Information* (Washington, DC, 1994).
16. Clotfelter and Cook, *Selling Hope*, 21.
17. *The Economist*, November 27, 1993, 39.
18. Hugh Muir, "Winning the Lottery's Jackpot: A Joy or a Burden?" *Electronic Telegraph*, December 14, 1994, 1, http://www.telegraph.co.uk.
19. Clotfelter and Cook, *Selling Hope*, 54.
20. *New York Times*, June 4, 1994, 24: 1.
21. *Dayton Daily News*, March 3, 1995, 1.
22. Jane Thynne, "Bottomley Defends Record £35m Lottery Prize as Great Fun," *Electric Telegraph*, January 5, 1996, 1, http://www.telegraph.co.uk.
23. Roger E. Brinner and Charles T. Clotfelter, "An Economic Appraisal of State Lotteries," *National Tax Journal*, 28, no. 4 (1975), 395–403.
24. *New York Times*, May 21, 1989, IV, 6:1.
25. North American Association of State and Provincial Lotteries, *Lottery Facts and Background Information*, 8 (Washington, DC, 1994).
26. North American Association of State and Provincial Lotteries, *Lottery Facts* (Cleveland, 1998).
27. Alan J. Karcher, "State Lotteries," *Society*, 29, no. 4 (May/June 1992), 52.
28. *Forbes*, January 23, 1989, 52–53.
29. Alan J. Karcher, *Lotteries* (New Brunswick: Transaction Publishers, 1992), xii.
30. *Forbes*, March 6, 1989, 17.
31. *Cash Explosion* broadcast, September 3, 1994.

32. *Columbus Guardian*, 2, no. 29 (July 21, 1994), 10.
33. *New York Times*, July 18, 1989, I, 1: 1.
34. Oregon Lottery, *Sports Action Nutshell: A Factsheet*, July 29, 1994.
35. Judith Michael, *Pot of Gold* (New York: Poseidon Press, 1992), 21.
36. Ibid., 61–62.
37. *New York Times*, January 13, 1993, B1: 2.
38. Ibid., B1: 12.
39. *New York Times*, March 31, 1994, C7: 1.
40. C. Wright Mills, "The Promise," from *The Sociological Imagination* (New York: Oxford University Press, 1967 [1959]), 6.

TWO

LOTTERIES IN
U.S. HISTORY

In 1607, the Virginia Company of London, started by a group of English merchants hoping to generate profits from a North American settlement, established a colony called Jamestown. Those people enlisted by the company to work in Jamestown spent little time preparing to sustain themselves in their new environment, but instead were pressured by the company to launch an immediate search for gold and to accumulate lumber, ore, tar, and any other potentially profitable exports. Almost a year later, when ships arrived to ferry the booty back to England, only a third of the original colonists were alive. Over the next several years the settlement was beset by disease, famine, fire, and dissension. Jamestown was generating little income for its investors, and funds to support it were desperately needed. In 1612, James I, the king of England, granted the Virginia Company a charter that permitted the establishment of a lottery to fund the struggling colony. The lottery was promoted throughout England and publicized by handbills containing the following stanza:

> It is to plant a Kingdom sure,
>   where savage people dwell;
> God will favor Christians still,
>   and like the purpose well.
> Take courage then with willingnesse,
>   let hands and hearts agree;
> A braver enterprize than this,
>   I thinke can never bee.[1]

By 1620, lottery proceeds provided almost half the revenues necessary for this colonial undertaking.[2]

Before the sixteenth century, the chance result from the casting of the "lot" was used primarily for making decisions during religious rituals, where drawing lots was used regularly to discover divine will. Games of chance, though, were largely condemned because they were believed to be a sacrilege and to encourage improvidence. However, changing economic and social systems in the sixteenth century created pressing financial needs. The privileged, engaged in the development of nation-states, were in need of revenues to administer, protect, and expand their empires—and to sustain their lives of luxury. In 1569 Queen Elizabeth of England chartered a lottery to bolster the exchequer. And, as in the case of nascent business enterprises like the Virginia Company, investment capital was needed.

The public demand for lotteries in this era was fostered by the decline of the medieval, agriculture-based feudal system, where one's position in society was determined largely by birth and tradition. With the rise of capitalism, formal caste-like social relations gave way as large numbers of people were pushed into the economic marketplace, forced to sell their labor at subsistence wages. The *society of status* was being replaced with a *society of contract* in which an economic free-for-all emerged.[3] Reflecting on early capitalism, Robert Heilbroner and Lester Thurow write:

> [T]he economic freedom of capitalism came as a two-edged sword. On the one hand, its new freedoms were precious achievements for those individuals who had formerly been deprived of the right to enter into legal contracts. For the up-and-coming bourgeois merchants, it was the passport to a new status in life. Even for some of the poorest classes, the freedom of economic contract was a chance to rise from a station in life from which, in earlier times, there had almost been no exit. But economic freedom also had a harsher side. This was the necessity to stay afloat by one's own efforts in rough waters where all were struggling to survive. Many a merchant and many, many a jobless worker simply disappeared from view.[4]

People seeking opportunities to improve their station in life, and those just trying to survive, created a considerable market for lotteries. Thus, lotteries were used to create finance capital and to boost state revenues, and they offered the masses of disenfranchised and exploited people a chance for better fortunes during the difficult years of early English capitalism.

Although the Virginia Company's profit-making venture at Jamestown ended in failure, a great deal of wealth was obtained from the American colonies. Most of this wealth, which accrued to the European aristocratic elite and the early capitalist entrepreneurs, resulted from the expropriation of Native American homeland and the exploitation of people who were indentured or enslaved. The British beneficiaries of the plundering of the Western Hemisphere, though, were reluctant to finance infrastructure development in the colonies, and lotteries became firmly rooted in North America as well. Throughout the colonial period, lotteries were necessary to raise funds to build ship landings, roads, bridges, churches, and schools. In the latter part of the nineteenth century, the newly liberated United States continued to practice unsavory ways of generating wealth and to concentrate it largely among the national elite. The new nation had few financial institutions, and capital for public works was scarce. Like the elite on the Continent, the U.S. elite were also reluctant to spread their wealth for public projects. So, in the 1790s a series of lotteries were held to fund improvements and construction in Washington, D.C. Between 1790 and the Civil War, lotteries were used to create revenues for forty-seven colleges, including Rutgers, Columbia, Brown, Dartmouth, Princeton, Yale, and Harvard.[5] Just as in England, private entrepreneurs also found lotteries to be a source of capital for the start-up and expansion of such enterprises as paper mills, blast furnaces, breweries, nail factories, and glass works.

Not surprisingly, many leaders of the period were critical of the pervasive presence of lotteries. In 1699 a group of Congregational ministers meeting in Boston denounced lotteries based on their concern that winners actually received only a small portion of the large sums collected. The ministers declared lotteries to be "a plain cheat upon the people."[6] Concerned with the moral consequences of lotteries, Congregational minister Cotton Mather wrote that same year:

> The undertakers in … a lottery only resolve to pillage the people of a considerable sum, and invite a number to assist them in their actions, in hopes of going shares with them in the advantage; and such is the corruption of mankind, that the mere hope of getting the riches of other men without doing the service of anything for it, will engage men to run the hazard of being losers.[7]

Opposition to lotteries was also expressed by merchants who complained that lotteries were "diverting large sums from regular commercial channels."[8] Colonial government officials began to express concern that lotteries were having a "harmful effect upon the lower classes.… Flushed with great expectations, they neglected their less exciting pursuits to loiter around the taverns where raffles commonly were held."[9]

These concerns, combined with growing allegations of lottery-related fraud and corruption in the early 1700s, led many colonial governments to enact laws requiring government approval before a lottery could be established. Still, despite the criticisms and problems, colonial lawmakers were in no position to outlaw lotteries altogether. Banks and other capital-producing institutions were as yet undeveloped, and taxation was an unpopular and laborious process. Manufactured goods were imported from England at substantial cost, draining the colonies of currency, and English law prohibited the issuing of lines of credit for the creation of additional currency. These factors resulted in a shortage of money and an atmosphere of general financial instability. Under these circumstances, lotteries played an essential role in creating capital for business development and public works. The importance of lotteries in the economic structure of the eighteenth century is reflected in their promotion by such notables as George Washington, Benjamin Franklin, William Fairfax, George Mason, and Thomas Jefferson.[10] In the absence of banks and other financial institutions, Jefferson observed,

> An article of property ... is sometimes of so large a value as that no purchaser can be found while the owner owes debts, has no other means of payment, and his creditors no other chance of obtaining it but by its sale at a full and fair price. The lottery is here a salutary instrument for disposing of it.[11]

While lotteries were used to raise revenues for public improvements, to fund new businesses, to build churches and schools and to dispose of large estates, they were also used to fund war efforts. The global struggles for empire that embroiled the colonists in the French and Indian War also brought considerable hardship and expense, and lotteries were used to subsidize colonial war-related activities. Moreover, the eventual struggle for independence from England was seriously hampered by the lack of a powerful central government, the mixed public support for the revolution and the dearth of money. The Revolutionary War was financed partially by lotteries, as was the postwar rebuilding. In the words of lottery historian John Samuel Ezell:

> [N]ot only did the ravages of war have to be repaired, but also material foundations for the youthful nation. Roads and bridges to open the back country; river channels and canals to transport market-bound produce; new industries to bolster the economy; churches and schools to tend to the inner man—those made money essential. Taxation alone was still not adequate, and facilities to consolidate small individual contributions were lacking. Neither were there stock or bond issues, and the lottery many times seemed the only resource. Thus cupidity, not patriotism, often financed the new nation's future.[12]

Under the Articles of Confederation, the agreement that bound the thirteen colonies from 1776 to 1789, each state created its own currency. This practice generated wild inflation and caused serious depreciation of the entire monetary system. Because leaders of the new nation feared that an excessive number of banks, and bank loans, would continue currency depreciation, the first commercial bank was not chartered in the United States until 1781. When the new constitution was ratified in 1789, the number had grown only to three,[13] and the early banks practiced very conservative money management.

Nascent capitalist financial institutions were slow to develop in the United States in part because the wealthy of the period were concerned that their investments and speculations would be devalued by depreciated currency. Thus, lotteries—drawing heavily from marginalized and disenfranchised people hoping to improve their lives—were used throughout the early to mid-nineteenth century to finance business development as well as government buildings, street paving, water systems, fire equipment, and other public needs. The great reliance on lotteries as an economic tool was noted by historian John Bach McMaster, who concluded that there was a lottery wheel in "every city and town large enough to boast a court-house and a jail."[14] While some religious opposition to the widespread use of lotteries continued, many congregations used lotteries to finance church construction.

Lottery Troubles in Europe

In Europe, those with more modest means were also tapped for the construction of churches, schools, and related projects. In sixteenth-century France, for example, lotteries were used to fund the church of Saint-Sulpice in Paris and the Military School of Paris. Religion was used, when possible, to promote and legitimate lotteries and to counter long-held disapproval of gambling. In one charitable lottery established to create dowries for impoverished but "virtuous women," the phrase "God has chosen you" was printed on winning tickets. The drawing was conducted on Palm Sunday, and Pope Sextus V granted the promoters of the lottery remission of sins.[15]

By 1776, facing a severe budget deficit, the state claimed the sole right to conduct lotteries and declared private lotteries unlawful. Leaders of the French Revolution, however, were highly critical of the state lottery on the grounds that it exploited the poor. One new public official called the lottery "a scourge invented by despotism to quiet the people by giving them false hope"; during a debate on the matter in the National Assembly one member decried the lottery as a "tax whose proceeds stem from folly or despair."[16] The revolutionary government abolished all lotteries in France in 1793. The moral high ground of the new government had eroded by 1799, however, when the state lottery was reinstituted after the government experienced budget problems and found itself losing revenues and currency as French citizens illegally played foreign lotteries.

The lottery survived in France until 1836, when it was halted by another temporary ban. As in the United States, French lottery detractors of the 1830s claimed that it harmed the poor and diverted resources from conventional business channels. One opponent argued at the Council of the Five Hundred (as the Parliament was then called):

> Ask this desolated mother whose children die of hunger; she will tell you: My husband was addicted to the lottery and we are left without resources. Ask this firm why it is bankrupt; the lottery is the cause.[17]

In seventeenth-century England lotteries were chartered by the crown for a variety of purposes, including funding the Virginia Company, as well as boosting the state treasury. Opposition to the lottery there began to develop in the middle of the seventeenth century, with critics charging that "the excitement of the lottery had demoralized business and industry" and that "the meaner sort of people are diverted from their work."[18] The preamble to the 1699 act of Parliament banning lotteries asserted that the lotteries had

> most unjustly and fraudulently got … great sums of money from the children and servants of several gentlemen, traders and merchants … to the utter ruin and impoverishment of many families.[19]

As in France, however, the ban on lotteries in England did not last. Beginning in 1709, the British Parliament approved lotteries to generate revenues for the state. It was not until a century later that a committee formed in the House of Commons to review the social effects of lotteries generated a report that was "full of horror stories about people for whom the lottery had proved to be their downfall."[20] As in France, a ban on lotteries was enacted in 1823, based on the legislature's findings that "their continuance corrupted the morals, and encouraged a spirit of Speculation and Gambling among the lower classes of the people."[21]

Decline of Lotteries in the U.S.

Not surprisingly, the masses of people in the United States in the eighteenth and early nineteenth centuries were supportive of lotteries. Although social and economic opportunities for white males in the thirteen colonies, and later in the new republic, were better than what many would have experienced in Europe, vast inequalities existed. In 1760, fewer than five hundred merchants in five colonial cities controlled most of the trade on the eastern seaboard and an enormous amount of land.[22] While there was a small middle class made up primarily of small business owners or professionals, the bulk of the free citizenry were poor freeholders, tenants, squatters, laborers, clerks and domestics who worked either as indentured servants or for paltry wages.[23] Dramatic disparity in wealth continued throughout the nineteenth century.[24] For example, the richest 4 percent of the population owned 49 percent of the wealth in New York City in 1829.[25] By 1845 that amount increased to 66 percent.[26] In most cities in the United States in the mid-nineteenth century, the richest 1 percent of the population possessed between 40 and 50 percent of the wealth, and the richest 10 percent owned between 80 and 90 percent.[27]

The importance of wealth in the colonies is reflected in a comment made in 1748 by New Yorker Cadwallader Colden, who complained that "the only principle of life propagated among young people is to get money and men are only esteemed according to ... the money they are possessed of."[28] Get-rich-quick ideals permeated the early nineteenth century, prompting an advisor to the U.S. War Department, John J. Albert, to write:

> The desire to grow rich, and to grow rich rapidly, are the besetting sins of our country.... If one is only successful, the means of acquiring it are not looked into, and if not too glaringly dishonest are rarely condemned. Look around you in the world and see what a crime it is to be poor.[29]

Lotteries presented an opportunity to change the conditions of one's life quickly, a change that for many must have seemed otherwise unlikely.

However, the acceptance of lotteries began to wane after the first quarter of the nineteenth century. Lotteries had grown so numerous and of such size that the integrity of the practices came to be seriously questioned. Allegations of fraud and corruption were supported by increasing evidence that large sums of lottery revenues were unaccounted for. For example, in 1831 an investigation of a lottery authorized by the state of Pennsylvania revealed that an effort to raise funds for infrastructure improvements yielded enormous profits for the lottery company. Of the $5 million generated in total sales, the state received just $27,000 while the lottery company took $800,000.[30] According to H. Roy Kaplan,

> Misrepresentations, swindles, and riggings became widespread. Even in colonial days abuses occurred, such as awarding inferior goods as prizes or manipulating drawings so that valuable items remained undrawn. Some promoters even fled before drawings were held. As lotteries grew bigger, so did the magnitude of the abuses.[31]

Moreover, like both the lottery detractors of a century earlier and those opposed to lotteries in France and England, critics argued that lotteries adversely affected lower-income people. Writing of nineteenth-century lotteries, John Bach McMaster notes:

> The time spent in making inquiries regarding [the lotteries] and in attending at the lottery offices, the feverish anxiety that seized on the adventurer from the day he bought his ticket, the depression and disappointment that so invariably followed the drawing, diverted the laborer from his work, weakened his moral tone, consumed his earnings, and soon brought him to pauperism.[32]

By 1834, Massachusetts, New York, Pennsylvania, Ohio, Vermont, Maine, New Jersey, Illinois, and New Hampshire had outlawed lotteries. Provisions prohibiting legislatures from authorizing lotteries were written into the constitutions of many states. In 1840, a group of citizens in Rhode Island, pressuring the legislature to abolish lottery activity in that state, presented a petition that summarized what had come to be the standard anti-lottery charges of the period. They maintained that:

> (1) lotteries were liable to the strongest objections that could be cited against gambling and were more dangerous than most forms because they were less offensive to decorum and less alarming to the conscience; (2) they presented the strongest temptations to fraud on the part of all concerned either in the drawing or sale of tickets; (3) they acted as a tax upon the community—a tax paid mainly by those who could least afford it; (4) they were the parents of much of the pauperism of the land; (5) success was hardly less fatal than failure, since the fortunate adventurer was never satisfied; and (6) they were especially mischievous in America because of the nature of its institutions and the prevalence of the get-rich-quick mania.[33]

Although fraud and exploitation of the poor were factors in the decline of lotteries in the mid-nineteenth century, they were nothing new, as critics had made similar complaints a century earlier. A more important factor in changing attitudes toward lotteries was the availability of other means of capital formation. Slowly, financial institutions were developing. By 1810, eighty-eight state-chartered banks were in operation providing money for business development and mortgages. By 1820 that number had grown to more than three hundred, and by 1860 more than fifteen hundred state banks existed.[34] The New York Stock Exchange had grown in size and legitimacy during the first half of the nineteenth century, and insurance and savings and loan associations supplemented the banks in mobilizing capital, reducing the necessity for lottery-generated funds.

By now, the bulk of the expenses of the federal government were being paid for by tariffs, excise taxes on alcohol, and proceeds from the sale of land. At the state level, various attempts were made at establishing income taxes, and, at both the state and local level, general property taxes were becoming the largest revenue source. The increasing size of economic institutions and concentration of economic power during the early to mid-nineteenth century were reflected also in the way lotteries operated. Small-scale, local lotteries were replaced with large, multi-state operations, and public confidence in these enterprises diminished as the incidence of irregularities and rigged drawings increased. Lottery-related machinations and fraud, coupled with the emergence of financial institutions that made more capital available, led to the decline of lotteries in the mid-nineteenth century. By the beginning of the Civil War, lotteries were legal in only three states, Delaware, Kentucky, and Missouri.

However, the decline of lotteries was not to last long. The Civil War created enormous financial needs in the South that were not easily provided for by existing economic institutions. While the war had produced industrial growth and relative prosperity in the North, it devastated several Southern states, where lotteries were revived out of financial necessity. Alabama, Georgia, and Mississippi reinstituted lotteries to help finance reconstruction; Louisiana had established a lottery earlier to fund the war effort. Some adventurous lottery promoters seized the opportunity to reestablish lottery participation in states where lotteries remained illegal.

A number of lottery enterprises evaded state prohibitions by calling themselves "gift companies," promoting lottery sales under the guise of selling merchandise.[35] The Mississippi Agricultural, Educational, and Manufacturing Aid Society was chartered by the state in 1867 to receive subscriptions, and sell and dispose of certificates of subscriptions which shall entitle the holders thereof to ... any lands, books, paintings, statutes, antiques, scientific instruments or apparatus, or any other property or thing that may be ornamental, valuable or useful ... [that may be] awarded to them ... by the casting of lots, or by lot, chance or otherwise.[36]

Chief Justice Waite of the U.S. Supreme Court commented that in the charter of this lottery company "there was an evident purpose to conceal the vice of the transaction by the phrases that were used."[37]

Responding to the public denunciation of these questionable enterprises, and after much debate, the United States Congress in 1868 made it illegal to sell lottery tickets by mail, and many states outlawed lotteries within their borders. The state-chartered lottery company in Mississippi filed suit, claiming that the state's constitutional amendment banning lotteries, ratified less than three years after the state in 1867 had granted the company a twenty-five-year license to operate, violated the U.S. constitution's prohibition on government actions impairing the obligation of contracts. The U.S. Supreme Court held that the power to regulate or ban lotteries was well within the state's police power, which extends to "all matters affecting the public health or public morals." Chief Justice Waite wrote of the "inherent vices" of lotteries, asserting

that they are demoralizing in their effects, no matter how carefully regulated, cannot admit of a doubt.... They are a species of gambling, and wrong in their influences. They disturb the checks and balances of a well ordered community. Society built on such a foundation would almost of necessity bring forth a population of speculators and gamblers, living on the expectation of what, "by the casting of lots, or by lot, chance or otherwise," might be "awarded" to them from the accumulations of others.[38]

Although Southern lotteries continued operating for some time, by 1878 opponents had successfully ended lotteries in every state but Louisiana, the site of the greatest lottery scandal of all. For three decades Louisiana sanctioned a state lottery operated by a private company that flourished despite repeated charges of fraud, theft, and widespread political corruption. Louisiana lottery tickets were hawked in almost every major city in the United States, and in its golden years the lottery company's net profit has been estimated at between $3 million and $5 million annually.[39] In the face of anti-lottery forces, lottery operators in Louisiana bribed state officials and manipulated elections to ensure the lottery's continuation. Numerous members of the Louisiana assembly were suspected of accepting bribes. Lottery historian George Sullivan notes:

> Some legislators resisted the temptation, but it was not easy. One J.M. McCann of Winn, Louisiana, a stern foe of the lottery, reported finding bundles of fresh currency under his hat every time he placed it down. Money dropped from windows at his feet. Once he attended a dinner for local politicians and discovered $20,000 in cash under his plate.[40]

A Louisiana representative to the United States House of Representatives, E. W. Robertson, remarked in 1882:

> Poor as I am, the lottery company cannot buy me, and as this question has entered into our politics, I propose to make it an issue in every canvass from governor down to constable. It has been charged that this lottery company controls the Legislature, and even members of Congress. Is it not, then, our duty to fight this despotism that is worse than hell itself?[41]

Despite the opposition to lotteries among many business leaders, religious organizations, and politicians, there was no lack of buyers for Louisiana lottery tickets, especially among the poor. Records from a New Orleans lottery shop showed that, within one hour, thirty-four people entered: eighteen women, six children and ten men. More than 65 percent of these customers were African American.[42] For women, whose economic opportunities were severely circumscribed, and for African Americans, who faced the onset of segregation and "Jim Crow" laws—enforced by violence—the lottery must have seemed the only chance available for a better life. One late-nineteenth-century writer visited a Louisiana lottery shop and offered an insight into the actions of ticket buyers:

> These tickets are placed on sale in some of the lowest dens in our large cities. In these places I have repeatedly seen women, young girls, and children standing, with trembling forms, waiting their turns, while the atmosphere about them was poisoned with the fumes of whiskey and tobacco, and filled with the foulest language, flowing from the lips of the veriest scoundrels lounging in these places.... Mental and moral demoralization follow the victim, and in proportion to the amount invested. The purchaser of lottery tickets, so soon as he has secured one, begins to speculate as to the probabilities of his holding the lucky number. He then begins to reason out the possibilities of his drawing a big prize. He bases his calculations upon his hopes rather than upon his chances.[43]

Some of the opposition to the lottery was based less on concern for the exploitation of the poor than on a concern that they were being distracted from "their responsibilities." One New Orleans clergyman asserted, "To send a servant with money to the market is virtually to send a portion of your money to the lottery," and "while the house-holder might wonder about his skimpy meal, the cook did not."[44] Religious organizations joined in denouncing the Louisiana lottery. In 1890 the Methodist Conference called the lottery a national disgrace and pledged to help end the enterprise; the Southern Baptists wished the Methodists "God speed" at their 1891 convention.[45]

In 1890 President Benjamin Harrison asked Congress for legislation that would put an end to lottery activity in the country. Lotteries, President Harrison said, "debauched and defrauded" the people of the United States.[46] Two months later Congress responded with legislation that banned "all letters, postal cards, pamphlets, circulars, tickets—anything at all having to do with the lottery—from the mails."[47] The profiteers behind the Louisiana lottery struggled on, attempting to promote lottery participation without the use of the mail. Congress responded in 1895 by making it illegal to transport any lottery material across state lines. By the end of the century the Louisiana lottery was effectively ended, as was virtually all lottery activity in the United States.

Lotteries in the Twentieth Century

By the start of the twentieth century the American economic system had changed considerably from the relatively open and expanding economy that had existed in the 1800s. There was still wide disparity in the distribution of wealth and a large segment of the population—including women, people of color, and people with disabilities—was largely excluded from the social and economic opportunities of the time. However, the opportunities for land ownership and business ventures that were available even to white males had begun to decline. With growing industrialization and urbanization and the development of large corporations, economic activity became increasingly concentrated and centralized, and entrepreneurial opportunities for the average citizen decreased. This gradual transformation within the economic system meant that one's potential for self-employment and economic independence declined as large corporations emerged, diversified, and began appropriating the economic activity that once was controlled mainly by smaller businesses. This change in the economic system also meant that important economic decisions that could effect entire communities, states, and even the nation were increasingly being made by smaller numbers of people.

During the first decade and a half of the twentieth century many people in the United States faced tremendous hardship. While a wealthy few, such as the Rockefellers, Carnegies, Vanderbilts, and Astors, lived opulent lives of conspicuous consumption, many residents of the growing U.S. cities experienced unemployment, low wages, poverty, poor housing, and poor sanitation. Many social reformers of the period increasingly placed responsibility for social ills on the capitalist system. While critics charged that greed and wrongful corporate practices underlay many of the nation's social and economic problems, defenders of the status quo countered by alleging that the poor were largely responsible for their own fate, due in no small measure to some form of mental deficiency.[48] Apologists for the system promoted a social Darwinist philosophy, claiming that society's "fittest" were in their rightful place at the top while the less fit properly occupied the slums. Immigrants, people of color, and people with disabilities were blamed for the existence of poverty, even though an 1890 study suggested that 1 percent of the population owned more property than the remaining 99 percent.[49] Structural arrangements notwithstanding, the state—serving its role as a primary legitimator and protector of wealth—transformed into public policy the explanations provided by the defenders of wealth by establishing restrictive immigration policies, while state governments legalized and promoted the forced sterilization of people defined as "defective." Although some dissension existed during this period, wealth continued to be esteemed and poverty, perhaps more than ever, became a source of disgrace.

Economic and social problems were overshadowed between 1917 and 1919 by the involvement of the United States in the First World War. To finance the war effort Congress enacted the War Revenue Act of 1917, which imposed steeply graduated taxes on individual and corporation incomes while also taxing inheritances. After the war, Andrew Mellon, the extraordinarily wealthy steel and aluminum tycoon who had become Secretary of the Treasury, devoted himself to cutting these taxes. Due in large part to his efforts, Congress cut individual and corporate income tax rates and the inheritance tax by half. The largest tax cuts were for wealthy individuals and corporations, measures that Mellon argued were necessary to fund growth and investment.[50]

Unfortunately, the deep-seated get-rich-quick mentality that was pervasive in the United States was not compatible with the kind of sound and responsible economic decisions and investments needed to create jobs and serve societal needs. Corporations worked to keep the cost of labor low, and the power of government frequently was used to weaken labor unions and to control striking workers. For example, in 1920, U.S. Attorney General A. Mitchell Palmer and his young aide, J. Edgar Hoover, coordinated the arrest of thousands of workers, citizens and noncitizens alike, for deportation or to face other charges. The majority were labor union officials and members. With no regard for due process of law, Palmer charged that many of the workers were communists, and hundreds were deported without hearings or trials.

The ability of big business to weaken labor and keep wages low created problems, however, because many in the workforce could not afford the goods the system was producing. The problem of the lack of a market for many manufactured goods was further compounded by the rampant speculation and stock swindles of the 1920s, which moved Harvard economist William Z. Ripley in 1926 to blast the "honeyfugling, hornswoggling and skulduggery" of corporate practices.[51] By the 1930s, ruinous practices by corporations and financiers played a primary role in the creation of the Great Depression.

Not surprisingly, the economic disaster of the 1930s altered the moral landscape and brought forth efforts to reestablish lotteries in the United States. In 1934, nearly four decades after Congress enacted legislation that essentially ended lotteries, Representative Edward A. Kenney from New Jersey introduced a bill authorizing the federal government to establish a lottery to meet the expenses of the Veterans Administration, which had been adversely affected by a 25 percent reduction in the federal budget.[52] The following is an excerpt from a House committee debate in 1934.

> Mr. Thom: Is not this lottery simply a sly attempt to shift the burden of taxation to the persons least able to bear that burden?
>
> Mr. Kenney: I do not agree with the gentleman.... I reiterate that all of our burdens are borne, in the last analysis, by the so-called "poor man"; and when he is out of employment and the CWA [Civil Works Administration] has to take care of him, our expenses are not met and our budget is not balanced....
>
> Mr. Boylan: Is there not also the possibility that the poor man by participating in this lottery may become a rich man?
>
> Mr. Kenney: ... Absolutely. It holds out to the forgotten man practically the only hope he has of becoming comfortable in the near future.[53]

Pro-lottery arguments appeared in such respected publications as the *New York World-Telegram*, the *Nation*, the *Saturday Review*, the *United States News*, and the *New York Herald Tribune*.[54] At the same time, a resolution was introduced in the New York legislature to legalize lotteries in the state to help New York City balance its budget. Similarly, bills to authorize a state lottery were introduced in Massachusetts, New Jersey, Pennsylvania, Maryland, Louisiana, Illinois, Maine, New Hampshire, Connecticut, California, and Nebraska.

Lottery opponents were quick to criticize these efforts. An article entitled "Lotteries are Both Wrong and Stupid" appeared in the *Christian Century* in 1934.

> A new craze for lotteries seems to be rampant. Apart from the ethics of it, trying to make money by investing in lottery tickets is one of the most idiotic forms of avarice ever invented.... It is even worse in times of depression than in periods of prosperity. To dangle glittering prizes before the eyes of men who are clutching at any straw to keep them afloat, is the most cruel kind of financial malpractice.[55]

A 1934 article in the *American City* entitled "Lotteries for Public Revenues—A Medieval Throwback" observed:

> We make progress slowly. Discredited institutions of one century, thought to have been permanently abolished after a long struggle, are revived in later centuries and the battle has to be fought all over again.[56]

The debate on the merits of reestablishing lotteries in the United States faded when President Franklin D. Roosevelt successfully pressed for tax increases. In 1935 Congress enacted what critics called a "soak-the-rich" scheme as President Roosevelt obtained the highest and most progressive peacetime tax rates in history.[57] While the new tax law did not come close to "soaking" the rich, it did shift a sizable portion of the still modest tax load onto the affluent and alleviated some of the financial crisis. However, it was the Second World War that actually pulled the U.S. out of economic turmoil, with the 1940s showing greater economic growth than any other decade in U.S. history. The war-driven mobilization of the economy saw the nation's real gross national product grow by 36 percent during the 1940s.[58]

The war devastated the infrastructures of most of the world's industrial powers, leaving the United States unchallenged as the most economically powerful nation in the world. Postwar production soared as the United States became the primary supplier of manufactured goods, and the 1950s were a time of "high and increasing affluence."[59] During the period of postwar prosperity the concentration and centralization of economic power in the United States that had begun at the turn of the century continued. By 1954, the largest 135 corporations in the

United States owned 45 percent of the nation's industrial assets—or nearly one-fourth of the manufacturing capacity of the entire world.[60] Writing in 1967, economist John Kenneth Galbraith observed:

> Seventy years ago the corporation was still confined to those industries—railroading, steamboating, steel-making, petroleum recovery and refining, some mining—where, it seemed, production had to be on a large scale. Now it also sells groceries, mills grain, publishes newspapers and provides public entertainment, all activities that were once the province of the individual proprietor or the insignificant firm. The largest firms deploy billions of dollars' worth of equipment and hundreds of thousands of men in scores of locations to produce hundreds of products.[61]

The largest corporations in the United States dominated the economy, largely controlled the market instead of being controlled by it, co-opted government decision-making, and utilized their power against the interests of the country.[62] So, while the economy was growing in the postwar years, the growth of corporate America began pushing many small enterprises out of business as giant firms diversified and centralized both manufacturing and retail operations. As a consequence, people came to rely increasingly upon corporations for both jobs and goods. The sociologist C. Wright Mills noted that small, independent entrepreneurs, whom he called the "old middle class," were eventually transformed:

> In the early nineteenth century ... probably four-fifths of the occupied population were self-employed enterprisers; by 1870, only about one-third, and in 1940, only about one-fifth, were still in this old middle class. Many of the remaining four-fifths of the people who now earn a living do so by working for the 2 or 3 percent of the population who now own 40 or 50 percent of the private property in the United States. Among these workers are the members of the new middle class, white-collar people on salary. For them, as for wage workers, America has become a nation of employees for whom independent property is out of range. Labor markets, not control of property, determine their chances to receive income, exercise power, enjoy prestige, learn and use skills.[63]

The postwar period of relative economic stability, while not offering great opportunities for self-sufficient employment, expanded labor markets, and many people found jobs. Although some people experienced economic prosperity in the postwar years in the United States, many experienced continued exploitation and poverty—injustices legitimated in part by racist, sexist, and classist ideology. In 1962 Michael Harrington called attention to the millions of people in the United

States who lived in poverty despite the country's economic growth and development. In his classic book *The Other America*, Harrington maintained that between forty and fifty million people were poor in the United States in the early 1960s. As Harrington observed, the prosperity created by the economic growth of the postwar era was maldistributed. The structural basis of persistent postwar poverty is obvious if the distribution of income in the United States between 1935 and 1970 is considered. In 1947 the poorest one-fifth of families in the U.S. received only 5 percent of the total national income. In 1970, after two decades of postwar economic expansion and affluence, the share of national income received by the poorest one-fifth had increased only to 5.4 percent.[64] Despite economic expansion, the distribution of economic resources in the United States was such that a large segment of the society was maintained in a state of relative deprivation.

While postwar economic expansion held off the legalization of lotteries during the 1940s and 1950s, participation in other games of chance saw dramatic development. This behavior is explained by Reuven Brenner and Gabrielle Brenner in the following way:

> [P]eople of all classes who have not previously gambled may decide to do so when they suddenly lose their wealth (for example, when they are fired, fear the increased probability of being unemployed, and so on).[65]

This statement is supported by the proliferation of gambling during the economic devastation of the 1930s. Bingo, first legalized in Massachusetts in 1931, became very popular and was used to fund charitable and religious organizations. Pari-mutuel betting followed, first legalized in New Hampshire, Ohio, and Michigan in 1933. While lotteries were illegal, "contests" and raffles of various design were widely used to promote products and businesses. Although they were much like lotteries, they were crafted in ways that effectively circumvented anti-lottery laws, usually by selling the right to participate jointly with another product. Chain letters were rampant and illegal numbers games prospered. Several public opinion polls of the period found considerable support for the reestablishment of lotteries. For example, in 1935 a poll conducted by *Fortune* magazine asked respondents, "Do you think that lotteries similar to the Irish Hospital Sweepstakes and conducted for charity and taxation should be allowed in this country?" Fifty-five percent of the respondents answered yes, 33 percent said no, and 12 percent were undecided.[66] A 1936 Gallup Poll found 59 percent approved of such a lottery,[67] and a 1941 poll by the American Institute of Public Opinion found that 51 percent of the respondents were in favor of a government lottery to pay the national debt.[68] The concept of lotteries was never buried too deeply in the nation's consciousness.

Factors Underlying the Legalization of Lotteries

While a large segment of the population was perhaps prepared to support lotteries because they represented a chance for economic security, if not the hope of wealth, there was also support for lotteries as an alternative to taxes. For example, in 1956 the Republican Party platform proposed the creation of a national lottery on the grounds that it would provide tax cuts for all taxpayers.[69] In 1963, during the period of relative national prosperity, New Hampshire's state school system was one of the poorest-funded in the country—due in no small measure to a resistance to the establishment of a state property or income tax. At that time the chief sources of income for the state were a gasoline tax, a tax on motor vehicle and drivers' licenses, and alcohol and cigarette taxes. The moral and ethical arguments against establishing a lottery in New Hampshire, discussed in Chapter 1, were drowned out by opposition to the creation of a state sales tax. New York lawmakers also resorted to lotteries in lieu of promoting increased taxes.[70] However, at the same time, other states rejected lottery proposals. Between 1963 and 1965, the legislatures in Florida, Rhode Island, Vermont, Connecticut, Maine and West Virginia voted down lottery bills.[71]

Resistance to the lure of lottery revenue began to wane as the "affluent society" faded in the late 1960s. In the 1970s the U.S. economy began to experience serious problems. The primary oil-producing countries formed a cartel, causing increases in the price of oil that contributed to double-digit inflation in the United States. More importantly, the seemingly endless U.S. economic expansion that followed the Second World War declined as the war-ravaged economies of Europe and Japan realized their inevitable recovery and emerged as global competitors. Much of the rebuilding in these nations used modern and efficient methods and equipment. Faced with the decision of whether to reinvest in new technology to remain competitive, or to divest and diversify, a number of powerful corporations chose the latter. Concomitantly, the United States experienced plant closings and significant corporate disinvestment, culminating in what has been called the "deindustrialization of America."[72] Due in part to the high degree of economic concentration and the fact that the United States had become a "nation of employees," the process of deindustrialization had dramatic consequences. Millions of people became unemployed. Between 1983 and 1987 alone, nearly ten million Americans lost their jobs due to plant closures and layoffs.[73] Faced with reduced opportunities for self-employment, and confronted with the loss of millions of jobs because of deindustrialization, people sought employment wherever they could find it. Speaking to the plight of unemployed workers, Michael Harrington observed:

> [T]he majority had either been driven from the labor force, were still unemployed, or had found new work at significantly lower pay. So it is that part-time work, sweat shops and "home work"—three forms of extreme exploitation in the early period of industrialism—have returned in the age of the computer.[74]

Others sought employment in the growing number of service-sector jobs. Of this trend, Robert Kuttner writes:

> As the economy shifts away from its traditional manufacturing base to high-technology and service industries, the share of jobs providing a middle-class standard of living is shrinking. An industrial economy employs large numbers of relatively well-paid production workers. A service economy, however, employs legions of keypunchers, sales clerks, waiters, secretaries, and cashiers, and the wages for these jobs tend to be comparatively low.[75]

In 1980, economist Lester C. Thurow observed, "[w]here the U.S. economy had once generated the world's highest standard of living, it is now well down the list and slipping farther each year."[76]

Economic centralization, developing global competition, and the resulting deindustrialization combined to produce a decline in the number of decent-paying jobs and in the economic status and quality of work experience of millions of working people. Economic insecurity increasingly fueled citizens' concern about how much local, state, and federal governments were taking from their paychecks. This middle-class outcry against high taxes occurred despite the fact that taxes in the United States are quite low compared to those in many other developed countries.[77] For years, affluent citizens had complained that the mildly progressive income taxes established by Roosevelt were unfair, even though most used loopholes that enabled them to avoid the established rates.[78] As a result, moderate-income people had been shouldering a disproportionate burden of public finance, generating a widespread anti-tax atmosphere.

This resistance to taxation culminated in the "taxpayer revolt" of the 1970s. In 1978, by a margin of 65 percent to 35 percent, California voters supported Proposition 13, a ballot initiative that cut taxes and cost the state approximately $5.5 billion in revenue.[79] Similar propositions passed in other states. George Peterson observes:

> The outburst of state tax relief between 1978 and 1980 saw twelve states reduce their general income tax rates and nine states index their income tax systems. Forty-three different states adopted new limitations on local property taxes or new property tax relief plans.[80]

The rhetoric of the tax revolt largely centered on ostensibly public-spirited criticism of the size of government, rather than more selfish complaints about the amount of taxes paid by individuals, and there was certainly little attention given to fairness in terms of the amount of taxes paid by the affluent when compared to other groups. Although most state and local taxes are regressive, meaning that lower-income people pay higher percentages of their incomes than higher-income people, voters supported tax cuts that applied to everyone. Thus, the tax revolt activity not only diverted attention from the fact that the affluent were not paying their fair share of taxes, but also benefited them by reducing their taxes even further. For example, the anti-tax sentiment was used to reduce the federal revenues from corporate income taxes. Although corporations accounted for 25 percent of federal tax receipts in the 1950s, the corporate share had fallen to just 12.5 percent in 1995.[81]

Faced with declining tax revenues due to industry and job losses and with intense resistance to raising taxes, state governments turned to lotteries to bolster strapped public coffers. New Jersey had begun lottery operations in 1970 and was joined by Michigan, Ohio, Maryland, Washington, Rhode Island, Maine, Connecticut, Massachusetts, Pennsylvania, Illinois, Vermont, and Delaware by 1978.

Further impetus for states to create lotteries was provided by the federal government. During the early 1980s President Reagan and his cadre of believers in "supply-side" economics sought to rejuvenate the economy. Following the general anti-tax atmosphere of the late 1970s, Reagan was successful in achieving tax cuts, although the primary beneficiaries were affluent individuals and corporations.[82] Tax cuts were coupled with business deregulation and dramatic increases in military spending. At the same time, the federal government cut domestic social programs, including those that provided low-income Americans with food, health care, affordable housing, and income support.

The Reagan-era policies exacerbated the already substantial polarization in the distribution of income and standards of living, a polarization into two societies that increasingly took on ethnic and racial overtones and disproportionately injured women and children.[83] By the end of the 1980s the share of income to the top 1 percent of Americans increased by $100 billion to $150 billion a year,[84] and the richest 1 percent of the population received nearly as much after-tax income as the entire bottom 40 percent.[85] The middle class in the United States shrunk while increasing numbers of the population experienced unemployment, poverty, hunger, and homelessness and crime rates skyrocketed.[86]

State and local governments also suffered tremendous additional economic strain during the 1980s. In addition to fiscal problems caused by the declining economy, state and local governments faced substantial cuts in federal programs. Federal revenue-sharing funds, community development block grants, mass transit programs, funds for education, housing subsidies, and other programs were substantially cut or eliminated, forcing state governments to assume the expense or scale back their programs. In the words of Alan J. Karcher, Speaker of the New Jersey Assembly from 1982 to 1986:

> The last budget submitted by President Carter to Congress provided that 14 percent of every dollar collected at the federal level be returned to the states and/or counties and towns in the form of federal aid. The amount of aid contained in the budget sent to Congress by President Reagan in 1988 was only a little over 9.5 percent of the total budget, $14 billion less than the amount of federal aid appropriated in 1981 in constant dollars.... The pressure on state officials represented by these numbers was enormous.... Taken as a whole, the evidence that emerges is rather compelling proof that a direct cause–effect relationship can be established between the policies of Reaganomics and the intensiveness of lottery activity.[87]

During the 1980s Arizona, California, Colorado, Florida, Idaho, Indiana, Iowa, Kansas, Kentucky, Missouri, Montana, Oregon, South Dakota, Virginia, West Virginia, Wisconsin, and the District of Columbia all established state lotteries.

The shortage of revenue continued to plague the states in the early 1990s. In February 1990 the New York Times noted, "More than half the states are battling serious budget problems as they approach the final months of the fiscal year."[88] In 1991 at least twenty-nine states faced potential deficits. Some took draconian measures, such as further cutting entitlement programs, laying off state employees, reducing funding to state colleges and universities, and closing down state government several days per month.[89] In the early 1990s five more states, Georgia, Louisiana, Minnesota, Nebraska, and Texas, established state lotteries. According to Duke University economists Charles T. Clotfelter and Philip J. Cook, "Revenue is the *raison d'être* of contemporary state lotteries. In every case where states have adopted this institution, potential revenues ... have been the principal selling point."[90]

Economic Forces and Lottery Activity

The historical development of lotteries in Europe and the United States, and their recent reemergence and proliferation, present a case study of the influence that economic forces can exert on social affairs—including the development of moral sentiment. Moreover, it supports the contention that one's opportunities—or lack thereof—and related experiences are shaped by the way in which society is organized, with the economic order conditioning other social arrangements. To begin with, it is interesting to note that human social affairs changed profoundly starting about ten thousand years ago as agricultural production began to replace a foraging existence. Agricultural society created opportunities for the accumulation of surplus wealth, and the social order eventually became hierarchical and largely tyrannical—resulting in the exploitation and oppression of the many by the few. Such material conditions generally have determined the life experiences of the majority of humanity for most of the past ten thousand years.

In the sixteenth and seventeenth centuries the privileged members of agricultural society, who relied heavily on the sword to maintain their power, came to be challenged economically and politically by nascent capitalist merchants and manufacturers. Over time, the new means of production, industrialization, released countless people from serfdom and slavery, since such arrangements were somewhat inconsistent with the emerging market economy. The new economic order instead compelled many to sell their labor—which remained devalued—in order to survive. However, similar to the arrangements of agricultural society, capitalism was hierarchical and tyrannical in its own way. While this evolving structural reformation brought new freedom to many, it also brought new dangers as the emerging system continued the practice of rewarding exploitation and concentrated surplus resources in the hands of a few. It was in this context that both incipient capitalist speculators and established aristocrats in sixteenth- and seventeenth-century Europe resisted wealth-sharing and turned to lotteries to further their self-interests.

New economic opportunities and exigencies contributed to the creation and maintenance of lotteries in both the North American colonies and the ensuing new nation. From the need to finance the Jamestown colony and nascent business enterprises to the need to create funds for roads, bridges, and schools in a new republic, lotteries were often the only means available to generate capital in the seventeenth, eighteenth, and early nineteenth centuries. They flourished despite strong criticisms from religious leaders and those concerned about the effects of lotteries on the poor. While lottery detractors were able to bring about some reform in the eighteenth century, lottery activity remained strong. It was only with the continued development of capitalism and the emergence of alternative methods of financing in the mid-nineteenth century that the concerns of lottery opponents about fraud, corruption, and exploitation of the poor could carry the day.

While economic factors were formidable, it is important to note the dialectical play among economic, political, religious, and social forces in lottery activity in the nineteenth century. Numerous religious leaders and organizations were against lotteries, and many business leaders also opposed lotteries because they believed they diverted funds from conventional uses and distracted working people from their tasks. From merchants and business proprietors to religious leaders, and from the Supreme Court to the President, lotteries were believed to promote immorality, corruptness, and a "debauched" citizenry. However, those who profited from lottery enterprises used their resources and influence to stave off or weaken restrictive legislation for years. Further, due to conditions of economic marginality for many, as well as the value and esteem given to wealth, the demand for lotteries was strong. A large segment of the population lived at a subsistence level and many—that is, women and people of color—were essentially precluded from improving their lives through the conventional channels of the day. All of these forces were important in the struggle over lotteries in the nineteenth century. Mainly, however, the eventual prohibition of lotteries, at both the state and the national level, was made possible by the development of more formal financial institutions that developed with industrial capitalism.

In the early decades of the twentieth century, a growing national economy and the creation of a national income tax during the First

World War helped to sustain the anti-lottery movement that had peaked in the 1890s. However, despite the denunciation of lotteries several decades earlier, the collapse of the economic system by the 1930s saw attempts to revive lotteries to raise desperately needed revenues. While lotteries were still considered harmful, other forms of gambling flourished during the Depression, when games of chance appealed to people's hopes of getting ahead and created resources for charities and churches and revenues for businesses and state governments. Much like in the eighteenth and early nineteenth centuries, when a lack of resources fueled lottery activity, churches and charities relied upon lottery revenues for operating funds. Raffles, bingo games, and other "contests" arose as a way to obtain resources during hard times. Businesses found these games of chance to be a very effective tool for marketing products and promoting retail establishments.

Although tax increases and the production needs of the Second World War spurred the economy, games of chance continued with broad public support. This is not surprising, since significant levels of poverty and economic marginality existed during the "affluent years." However, a serious discussion of lotteries as a source of public revenue did not emerge again for more than two decades.

Although the 1940s, 1950s, and early 1960s were a period of economic expansion, the refusal of New Hampshire residents to establish an income or sales tax in the face of a growing population and greater need for state services prompted the creation there of the first modern state lottery in 1964. Indeed, the general resistance of the public to new or increased taxes played no small role in the revenue problems that plagued state governments and opened the door to lotteries. Resistance to taxation was itself partially driven by declining economic conditions that were rooted in global economic competition and de-industrialization. This economic distress was compounded by state and federal tax cuts and drastic reductions in federal assistance to both individuals and state governments.

Recall that, in the cases of New Hampshire and New York, ethical and moral arguments against the revival of lotteries were abundant. Some people were aware of the nation's history with lotteries and concerned about their "demoralizing" and "debauching" effects. Similar arguments were raised in every state where lotteries were legalized. However, these ethical issues about appropriate ways to raise public revenue were largely eclipsed by economic pressures.

Why Do People Play Lotteries?

Many maintain that lotteries are primarily a form of recreation and entertainment and exist largely because people enjoy them. It is estimated that, in countries where some forms of gambling are legal and available, 80 to 90 percent of the population participate. However, two-thirds of those who gamble are infrequent participants who only occasionally buy a raffle ticket, fill out a "sweepstakes" form, or join an office sports pool.[91] Only about one-third of the adult population bets regularly each week.[92] Sociological theories about gambling have generally maintained that gambling is the result of some form of human dissatisfaction or deprivation.[93] It has been theorized that games of chance persist in Western industrialized society because they provide an outlet for the frustration of those who perceive that skill and hard work have no power to aid their chances of achieving success.[94] Edward Devereux maintains that gambling is a behavior rooted in the human endeavor to cope with uncertainty. In a capitalist society that emphasizes the work ethic and self-determination but that provides only limited opportunities, gambling serves two goals. It provides a potential means to improve one's economic status, while the subjective experience offers some satisfaction in the face of general frustration.[95] Research has generally supported the notion that the motivation to gamble is related to uncertainty and frustration. A study of patrons at a New England bar suggested that gamblers were attempting to exercise some control over their fate,[96] and a study of English coal miners found that

> the miners' motives for gambling were based on the knowledge that escape from the limitations of their life, the insecurity of the heavy, dirty, dangerous work, could not come from saving money but only from a really big win.[97]

Similarly, a study in Sweden found that gamblers were more dissatisfied with their job prospects and incomes than nongamblers.[98]

Others suggest, however, that gambling constitutes entertainment because of its social aspect. Race tracks and casinos offer opportunities for social interaction as gamblers consult with one another, form judgments, and enjoy the thrill of the event. While some researchers question the importance of the social component of actual gambling behavior, lotteries are largely viewed as "subjective private affairs not necessarily associated with cognitive skills or social interaction."[99] Reflecting on the assertion that state lotteries are a form of entertainment, Alan J. Karcher writes:

Visit the most distressed area of your state's poorest city and you will quickly witness what the lotteries in America have become. Look into the faces of those who line up at the terminals to buy tickets, counting the change in their pockets as the devout count the beads on a rosary. The tickets that they buy tax their dreams and their hopes. If this is really entertainment, why does no one seem amused? If this is recreation, then why is the mood so sullen and abject?[100]

Further evidence about the relationship between troubled economic conditions and the prevalence of games of chance comes from a sales promotion agency that specializes in sweepstakes. In 1981, the *New York Times* advertising columnist wrote about a sales promotion agency that specialized in sweepstakes promotions:

Not everyone is rooting for President Reagan's efforts on behalf of the economy. Take Jeffrey P. Feinman, President of Ventura Associates, for example. He says that his business is countercyclical, "in exact disproportion to the economy." ...

Those harassed automobile companies, pressed to fill showrooms, want sweepstakes that bring elusive customers in to see if they are among the well-promoted, preselected winners.

And packaged goods companies—the biggest believers in, and supporters of, advertising—are turning to it more and more.... Mr. Feinman believes that "the chance to win a dream can change a habit pattern."[101]

The brief review of lottery history undertaken earlier in this chapter supports the purported linkage between economic uncertainty and lottery participation. People with few opportunities or resources have always constituted a fertile market for lotteries, and concerns about their effect on such people have been the basis for historical opposition to lotteries both in the United States and in Europe. The relationship between economic insecurity and lottery play was assumed by Representative Kenney in 1934 when he said the lottery "holds out to the forgotten man practically the only hope he has of becoming comfortable in the near future." Moreover, millions of people who do have an acceptable level of economic security may feel trapped in a tedious, strenuous, or dangerous job. In an era of high economic concentration and dehumanized industry, there are fewer opportunities for rewarding, self-determining work, especially work that can provide the practical necessities of a decent wage, health care, and a pension plan. It is easy to see why even those who are not on the edge economically are still motivated by economic conditions to try their hand at the lottery.

Thus, while the reemergence of lotteries in the United States should be considered in the context of "consumer demand," there is evidence to suggest that economic frustration, insecurity, and despair are greater factors than entertainment in the demand for lottery games. Thus the public "demand" for lotteries is the product of an interplay between the compelling, even coercive, economic and social arrangements of one's times and the resulting concerns about one's economic circumstances, or survival. Moreover, in a society like the United States where wealth is prized, laboring is devalued, and poverty is denigrated, it is not surprising that people with few resources invest much hope, and no small part of their meager resources, in lotteries.

In the case of lotteries, both the economic policy and the values underlying it are deeply conditioned by economic circumstances. Recall that repeated moral challenges to the existence of lotteries, in the United States and abroad, resulted only in temporary bans or government regulation, but that lotteries reemerged or continued, moral arguments notwithstanding. Indeed, this example supports the contention that the "chill sting of penury"[102] can have a powerful impact upon both individual and societal conceptions of what is good or bad and how material necessities should be realized.

Finally, it is important to note that the economic conditions that contributed to the proliferation of lotteries earlier in the nation's history and the economic conditions that fostered their recent reemergence are different in an important respect. During the period of nascent capitalism in the seventeenth, eighteenth, and early nineteenth centuries, institutions for the generation and distribution of capital were undeveloped. Thus, early lotteries were more of an economic imperative for both public and private enterprises.

As capitalism grew, so did the number and type of financial institutions, and large corporations also developed the ability to generate internally much of the capital they needed for expansion. By the late twentieth century, institutions and processes for creating investment capital were very well developed—so why the need for lotteries? The answer lies in the fact that contemporary financial institutions, shaped by the forces of monopoly and global capitalism, serve the interests of private business far better than they serve the public sector. Today's lotteries are not used to fund business enterprise, although they may indeed generate a great deal of additional investment capital. Instead, during a time of corporate restructuring and increasing concentration of privately held wealth, lotteries have been created to support strapped *governments*. Although a more equitable and rational form of capitalism would be quite capable of generating the resources needed for schools, social services, and other public-sector needs, the managed but largely unrestrained capitalism of today precludes adequate funding of these public needs. Marxists have long maintained that the potential of industrialization to benefit the masses of the world's people was undermined by the opportunities that capitalism presented for the pursuit of individual wealth and power. As Galbraith observed, the goals of large corporations in the twentieth century have been incompatible with the nation's interests. Exploitation in one form or another, in which a relatively small group controls the many, has characterized Western society for the past ten thousand years. Today's powerful individuals—increasingly, with the use of the business corporation—have been able to exert a strong influence over economic, social, and political arrangements, not the least of which has been tax policy. The resulting relatively low rates of taxation actually paid by affluent individuals and corporations, coupled with deindustrialization and related self-interested actions by the controllers of wealth, have contributed to an economic crisis for state governments, providing fertile conditions for the revival of lotteries. Thus, it has been economic arrangements characterized by the persistence of unequal power and maldistribution of wealth, not undeveloped financial institutions, that contributed to the reemergence of lotteries in the twentieth century. The role of the state in creating the economic and social conditions that led to the reemergence of lotteries, and in establishing and promoting them, is the topic of the next chapter. The first part of the chapter will focus on questionable lottery-related state policies. The second part will place lotteries in the context of an examination of the role of the state and the function it performs for late-twentieth-century capitalism.

Notes

1. George Sullivan, *By Chance a Winner: The History of Lotteries* (New York: Dodd, Mead & Co., 1972), 13.
2. Ibid.
3. Robert L. Heilbroner, *The Making of Economic Society: Revised for the 1990s*, Eighth Edition (Englewood Cliffs, NJ: Prentice Hall, 1989), 37.
4. Robert L. Heilbroner and Lester C. Thurow, *Economics Explained* (Englewood Cliffs, NJ: Prentice Hall, 1982), 9.
5. H. Roy Kaplan, "The Social and Economic Impact of State Lotteries," *The Annals of the American Academy of Political and Social Science*, July 1984, 92.
6. John Samuel Ezell, *Fortune's Merry Wheel: The Lottery in America* (Cambridge, MA: Harvard University Press, 1960), 18.
7. Ibid.

8. Ibid., 19.

9. Ibid., 20.

10. Sullivan, *By Chance a Winner*, 20–21.

11. Ibid., 14.

12. Ezell, *Fortune's Merry Wheel*, 69.

13. Susan Previant Lee and Peter Passell, *A New Economic View of American History* (New York: W.W. Norton, 1979), 110.

14. John Bach McMaster, *History of the People of the United States: From the Revolution to the Civil War* (New York: Noonday Press, 1964); cited in Ezell, *Fortune's Merry Wheel*, 177.

15. Reuven Brenner and Gabrielle Brenner, *Gambling and Speculation: A Theory, a History, and a Future of Some Human Decisions* (New York: Cambridge University Press, 1990), 9.

16. Ibid., 212.

17. Ibid., 213.

18. Ibid., 10.

19. Ezell, *Fortune's Merry Wheel*, 9.

20. Brenner and Brenner, *Gambling and Speculation*, 11–12.

21. Ibid., 12.

22. Michael Parenti, *Democracy for the Few*, Sixth Edition, (New York: St. Martin's Press, 1995).

23. Ibid.

24. Leonard Beeghley, *Social Stratification in America: A Critical Analysis of Theory and Research* (Santa Monica, CA: Goodyear Publishing Company, 1978), 207–8.

25. E. Pressen, "The Egalitarian Myth and the American Social Reality: Wealth, Mobility and Equality in the 'Era of the Common Man,'" *American Historical Review*, 76, no. 4 (1971), 1022.

26. Ibid.

27. G. D. Lillibridge, *Images of American Society: A History of the United States*, Volume 1 (Boston: Houghton Mifflin, 1976), 242.

28. Ibid., 65.

29. Ezell, *Fortunes's Merry Wheel*, 185–86.

30. Mary Beth Norton, David M. Katzman, Paul D. Escott, Howard P. Chudacoff, Thomas G. Paterson, William M. Tuttle, Jr., and William J. Brophy, *A People and A Nation: A History of the United States* (Boston: Houghton Mifflin, 1991) 221.

31. Kaplan, "The Social and Economic Impact of State Lotteries," 93.

32. McMaster, *History of the People of the United States*, 216.

33. Ezell, *Fortune's Merry Wheel*, 221–22.

34. Jonathan Hughes, *American Economic History*, Second Edition (Glenview, IL: Scott, Foresman & Co., 1987), 199.

35. Ezell, *Fortune's Merry Wheel*, 235.

36. *Stone* v. *Mississippi*, 101 U.S., 814, 817 (1880).

37. Ibid.

38. Ibid., 818, 821.

39. Sullivan, *By Chance a Winner*, 56.

40. Ibid.

41. Anthony Comstock, *Traps for the Young* (New York: Funk & Wagnalls, 1884), 65.

42. Ezell, *Fortune's Merry Wheel*, 250.
43. Comstock, *Traps for the Young*, 59–60.
44. Ezell, *Fortune's Merry Wheel*, 250.
45. Ibid., 259.
46. Sullivan, *By Chance a Winner*, 57.
47. Ibid., 58.
48. David Nibert, "The Political Economy of Disability," *Critical Sociology*, 21, no. 1 (1995), 59–80.
49. C. B. Spahr. *The Present Distribution of Wealth in the United States.* 1896, cited in Harold U. Faulkner, *The Quest for Social Justice: 1898–1914* (Chicago: Quadrangle Books, 1971), 21.
50. Richard N. Current, T. Harry Williams, Frank Freidel and Alan Brinkley, *American History: A Survey. Volume II: Since 1865*, Sixth Edition (New York: Alfred A. Knopf, 1983), 705.
51. Samuel Eliot Morrison, *The Oxford History of the American People, Volume Three* (New York: New American Library, 1972), 285.
52. Helen M. Muller, *Lotteries*, Vol. X, No. 2 of the Reference Shelf Series (New York: H. W. Wilson Company, 1935), 54.
53. Ibid., 54–55.
54. Ibid., 6.
55. Ibid., 104.
56. Ibid., 108–10.
57. Current et al., *American History: A Survey*, 764.
58. Lester C. Thurow, *The Zero-Sum Society: Distributions and the Possibilities for Economic Change* (New York: Penguin Books, 1983 [1980]), 8.
59. John Kenneth Galbraith, *The Affluent Society* (Boston: Houghton Mifflin, 1958), 334.
60. Adolph A. Berle, Jr., *The 20th Century Capitalist Revolution* (New York: Harcourt, Brace and Co., 1954), 25.
61. John Kenneth Galbraith, *The New Industrial State* (Boston: Houghton Mifflin, 1967), 1.
62. Ibid.
63. C. Wright Mills, *White Collar: The American Middle Classes* (New York: Oxford University Press, 1951), 63.
64. Harold R. Kerbo, *Social Stratification and Inequality: Class Conflict in Historical and Comparative Perspective*, Second Edition (New York: McGraw-Hill, 1991), 33.
65. Brenner and Brenner, *Gambling and Speculation*, 22.
66. Ibid., 84.
67. Ibid.
68. Ezell, *Fortune's Merry Wheel*, 276.
69. Ibid., 277.
70. Charles T. Clotfelter and Philip J. Cook, *Selling Hope: State Lotteries in America* (Cambridge, MA: Harvard University Press, 1989), 143.
71. Ibid., 144.
72. See Barry Bluestone and Bennett Harrison, *The Deindustrialization of America: Plant Closings, Community Abandonment and the Dismantling of Basic Industry* (New York: Basic Books, 1982).
73. Joe R. Feagin and Robert Parker, *Building American Cities: The Urban Real Estate Game*, Second Edition (Englewood Cliffs, NJ: Prentice Hall, 1990), 39.

74. Michael Harrington, *The Next Left: The History of a Future* (London: I. B. Tauris, 1987), 83.

75. Robert Kuttner, "The Declining Middle," *Atlantic Monthly*, July 1983, 60–72.

76. Thurow, *The Zero-Sum Society*, 3.

77. Charles R. Hulten and June A. O'Neill, "Tax Policy," in *The Reagan Experiment*, ed. John L. Palmer and Isabel V. Sawhill (Washington, DC: The Urban Institute Press, 1982), 101.

78. See Philip Stern, *The Rape of the American Taxpayer* (New York: Random House, 1973).

79. Robert Kuttner, *Revolt of the Haves: Tax Rebellions and Hard Times* (New York: Simon & Schuster, 1980), 66.

80. George E. Peterson, "The State and Local Sector," in *The Reagan Experiment*, ed. Palmer and Sawhill, 184.

81. U.S. Bureau of the Census, *Statistical Abstract of the United States: 1997*, 117th edition (Washington, DC, 1997), 342.

82. See Kevin Phillips, *The Politics of Rich and Poor: Wealth and the American Electorate in the Reagan Aftermath* (New York: Random House, 1990).

83. See Andrew J. Winnick, *Toward Two Societies: The Changing Distribution of Income and Wealth in the United States Since 1960* (New York: Praeger, 1989); see also Ruth Sidel, *Women and Children Last: The Plight of Poor Women in Affluent America* (New York: Penguin Books, 1992).

84. See Phillips, *The Politics of Rich and Poor*.

85. Center on Budget and Policy Priorities, *Drifting Apart: New Findings on Growing Income Disparities Between the Rich, the Poor, and the Middle Class* (Washington, DC, 1990).

86. See Denny Braun, *The Rich Get Richer: The Rise of Income Inequality in the United States and the World* (Chicago: Nelson-Hall, 1991); see also Kenneth J. Neubeck, *Social Problems: A Critical Approach*, Third Edition (New York: McGraw Hill, 1991).

87. Alan J. Karcher, *Lotteries* (New Brunswick, NJ: Transaction Publishers, 1992), 20–21.

88. *New York Times*, February 25, 1990, 1.

89. Priscilla Painton, "A New Pragmatism," *Time*, March 4, 1991, 50–51.

90. Clotfelter and Cook, *Selling Hope*, 215.

91. Mark G. Dickerson, *Compulsive Gamblers* (New York: Longman, 1984), 18.

92. Ibid.

93. Ibid., 22.

94. Roger Callois, *Man, Play and Games* (New York: Free Press, 1962).

95. Edward Devereux, *Gambling and the Social Structure: A Sociological Study of Lotteries and Horse Racing in Contemporary America*, Ph.D. dissertation, Harvard University, 1949.

96. I. K. Zola, "Observations on Gambling in a Lower-Class Setting," in *The Other Side: Perspectives on Deviance*, ed. Howard Becker (New York: Free Press, 1964).

97. Norman Dennis, Fernando Henriques and Clifford Slaughter, *Coal is Our Life: An Analysis of a Yorkshire Mining Community* (New York: Tavistock Publications, 1969), cited in Mark G. Dickerson, *Compulsive Gamblers* (New York: Longman, 1984), 23–24.

98. Nechama Tec, *Gambling in Sweden* (Totowa, NJ: Bedminster Press, 1964).

99. Dickerson, *Compulsive Gamblers*, 25.
100. Karcher, *Lotteries*, 16.
101. Philip H. Dougherty, "His Specialty is Selling the End of the Rainbow," *New York Times*, June 4, 1981, IV, 16: 1.
102. Karcher, *Lotteries*, 19.

THREE

LOTTERIES AS
QUESTIONABLE STATE POLICY

Forest Park is a large metropolitan park located in the west end of St. Louis. There is an area in the park where people who are homeless frequently spend the night. In this area, one can readily find scratched and discarded instant lottery tickets. People without a home, hoping to turn a precious few dollars into $100, $500, or $1,000, ended up handing a substantial portion of their meager resources over to the state of Missouri as *tax*.

Is the lottery really a tax? A tax is essentially money collected by a government to be used for public purposes. If the public does not think of state lotteries as taxation, it is because state officials cultivate this lack of awareness. Former New Jersey state legislator Alan J. Karcher observes:

> Lottery spokespersons seldom, if ever, refer to the lottery as a tax. In lottery parlance, euphemisms such as "take out" describe revenues generated by lotteries.... Lottery advocates have devised other euphemisms to shield the playing public from realizing they are being taxed. Ticket buyers are always referred to as "players," never as taxpayers.[1]

Duke University professors Clotfelter and Cook note that lottery profits "are no less useful than revenues that are labeled taxes, so it is altogether appropriate to label them implicit taxes."[2] Indeed, state lotteries are frequently referred to as a "painless tax," because the general public largely supports lotteries and the additional public revenues they generate without the complaints that accompany other forms of taxation.

Are state lotteries a *fair* form of taxation? What is fair taxation? A classical answer to the question was developed by Adam Smith in the *Wealth of Nations*. Smith believed:

The subjects of every state ought to contribute toward the support of the government, as nearly as possible, in proportion to their respective abilities; that is, in proportion to the revenue which they respectively enjoy under the protection of the state ....[3]

How do state lotteries stand up to Smith's criteria? Do people with lower incomes give more in proportion to their incomes to the state through the "painless tax" than people with higher incomes?

A 1977 study by the Connecticut State Commission on Special Revenue found the state's daily numbers game attracted primarily the poor, the chronically unemployed, and the less educated, while those with college degrees and incomes over $25,000 largely ignored the state's various forms of lottery games.[4]

Clotfelter and Cook also found lottery participation to be disproportionately concentrated among people with lower incomes.[5] Using data from a Gallup survey of Maryland residents in 1984, they compared average lottery expenditures by all adults in five income groupings with the average for the 20 percent in each group who spent the most on the lottery. In every case the top 20 percent spent more than three times the average for the entire group. Especially revealing was the very heavy play among the most active players in the lowest-income group. Clotfelter and Cook's findings are illustrated in Table 3.1, which shows that the most active 20 percent in the $10,000-and-under group spent an average of about $32 per week on the lottery. In addition, a study conducted by Daniel Suits on lottery play in Michigan during fiscal year 1979–80 found that the proportion of family income spent on lottery tickets declined almost 12 percent for every 10 percent increase in per capita income.[6]

Lottery critics complain that state lotteries are unfair largely because they constitute a *regressive* form of taxation, defined as a tax that takes a larger percentage of the income of lower-income citizens than of those with higher incomes. In a 1977 study of tax regressivity, Daniel Suits found that state lotteries were two to three times more regressive than sales taxes.[7] In a 1979 study of Maryland's daily numbers game, Charles T. Clotfelter concluded that the Maryland lottery "appears to be increasing the regressivity of state revenue structures."[8] Other studies during this period produced similar findings,[9] prompting an essay in *Business Week* proclaiming that state lotteries were part of a tax structure that constituted a "low blow to the poor."[10]

As state lotteries developed, research studies continued to provide evidence that they are regressive and that this regressivity is increasing.

Table 3.1 Differences in lottery play within income classes, Maryland, 1984

Annual income	Average weekly expenditure ($)	
	All adults	*Top 20% of adults*
Under $10,000	7.30	32.56
$10,000 to $15,000	5.37	21.85
$15,000 to $25,000	2.99	12.15
$25,000 to $50,000	3.21	14.70
$50,000 and more	2.57	12.48

Source: Charles T. Clotfelter and Philip J. Cook, *Selling Hope: State Lotteries in America* (Cambridge, MA: Harvard University Press, 1989), 143.

A 1992 study of lottery play among 3,200 Oregon residents found that "lottery play represented a heavier burden for the poor in that a larger proportion of household expenditures are consumed by purchasing tickets,"[11] and a 1995 study of 701 Indiana residents found increasing levels of regressivity (see Figure 3.1). The authors of this study write:

> [T]he lottery is quite regressive, and this regressivity has increased with time. Among all persons in the lowest income category, total play in 1992 accounted for 1.78% of their total annual gross income, and 4.21% of the gross annual income of players only. Total annual lottery expenditures among the lowest-income respondents who play the lottery was $631.28 per year.... In 1992, 22.6% of lottery expenditures were accounted for by individuals in the lowest income category, an increase from 13.0% in 1988.[12]

This is troubling, since it means that poorer people are bearing, increasingly, the brunt of the "painless tax." This raises serious concerns about the *fairness* of lotteries as a method of raising public funds. Those who are least able to afford it are disproportionately bearing the burden of state budget problems. According to a state senator from Maryland, "lotteries place an inordinate burden on the poor to finance state government."[13]

In Canada, David Barrett, Premier of British Columbia from 1972 to 1976, expressed regret for his earlier support of the provincial lottery there. "It's simply a regressive and unfair form of taxation that lower-income people pay. We hadn't intended it that way, but that is the way it has worked out."[14] In the U.K., Stephen Hawking, the eminent mathematician and author of the best-selling *A Brief History of Time*, called

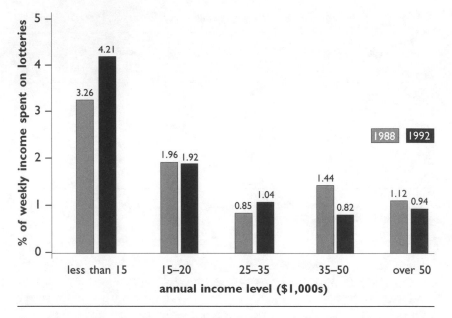

Source: Maureen Pirog-Good and John L. Mikesell, "Longitudinal Evidence of the Changing Socio-Economic Profile of a State Lottery Market," *Policy Studies Journal*, 23, no. 3 (1995), 454.

Figure 3.1   Indiana lottery players' weekly lottery expenditures as a percentage of their gross income, 1988 and 1992

lotteries "shabby and sleazy" and stated, "I object to the National Lottery because it takes money from those who are least able to afford it."[15] Thus, a lottery is not a tax that is generated in "proportion to the revenue" that individuals in society receive and, evaluated by Adam Smith's criteria, is decidedly unfair.

Lotteries as a fund-raising tool are also criticized because they offer states a very low rate of return compared to other forms of taxation, due in large part to the high ratio of administrative costs to dollars raised. Gary Becker, Professor of Economics and Sociology at the University of Chicago, observes:

> Lotteries have replaced "numbers" as the favorite method of gambling among the poor.... But only about half the amount wagered on lottery tickets is returned as prizes. From 30% to 45% of the revenue from lotteries, depending on the state, is tax. Why should states tax so heavily the pleasures poor bettors get from dreaming of a better life with less drudgery?

It is impossible to justify on equity grounds the heavy taxation of lotteries.... Even though the federal and many state governments are looking for additional state revenues to cut their budget deficits, they have shied away from raising taxes on groups that offer strong political opposition. Companies often use their political clout to keep down the taxes on their products.[16]

State Advertising of Lottery Products

Defenders of state lotteries respond to the regressivity issue by pointing out that lottery participation is strictly voluntary. They proclaim that it is people's own decision to spend their money on lottery tickets. Certainly, it is true that no one is forced to buy lottery tickets. However, the states provide considerable encouragement for people to do so, and they have not overlooked people with low incomes in their efforts. In 1986 a Chicago church organized a boycott of the Illinois lottery because of its advertising in poor neighborhoods,[17] and in 1989 local officials from several Virginia communities complained to state government officials that some lottery advertising "has the effect of inducing many citizens of limited or no income into playing the lottery."[18] In 1979 a study by the Delaware Council on Gambling Problems discovered that

[T]he State Lottery Commission has purposely placed its lottery machine locations in the poorest areas where there are the highest unemployment figures, the lowest standards of living and the highest percentage of welfare recipients.[19]

The study found no lottery machines in the highest-income areas of the state, one machine for every 17,774 people in upper-income areas, one for every 5,031 people in lower middle to middle income areas, and one for every 1,981 people in the poorest areas.[20]

Lottery promoters also actively target people of color. For example, a 1989 investigative report on the Missouri lottery revealed that a high percentage of its print advertising budget was spent on black newspapers. In the St. Louis area 71 percent of its print media budget was spent on four black newspapers; in Kansas City, the lottery spent 81 percent of its print budget on three black newspapers and one Hispanic paper. These advertisements were designed to both promote and legitimize the lottery in minority communities. A reporter for the St. Louis *Riverfront Times* observed:

For three weeks out of every month in each of the black newspapers, "Real Winners" ads highlight individuals in different facets of community life. For example, the three-quarter page ad in the March 8–14 *St. Louis American* highlighted three blacks who work in the engineering/technology field in St. Louis. All three participate in community programs for youth by being role models or tutors. Below the ad runs this caption: "The Missouri lottery, like these Real Winners, contributes to the strength of our community."[21]

Such heavy promotion of the lottery in minority communities is paying off. Clotfelter and Cook's study of lottery play in Maryland showed that 41 percent of blacks spent $10 or more per week on the lottery, compared to only 8 percent of whites. Similarly, a 1989 study by the Institute for Policy Research at the University of Cincinnati found that blacks were more likely than whites to play the lottery, with 33 percent playing every week compared to 21 percent of whites.[22]

It has been argued that state government promotion of lotteries, using all the gimmicks, schemes, and marketing methods of modern advertising, is a questionable government practice. Using such slogans as "If you don't play, you can't win," "Play your hunch, you could win a bunch," and "All you need is a dollar and a dream," state governments continuously seek to increase participation in their lotteries. One Washington State lottery winner proclaims in a musical testimonial, "Now I walk the streets of paradise." An Illinois ad pictured a man scoffing at people investing in savings bonds and insisting that winning the lottery is the only way an ordinary person can become a millionaire.[23]

Who regulates state lottery advertisers? They regulate themselves. In 1975 the National Association of State and Provincial Lotteries developed an Advertising Code of Ethics. Portions of the Code are as follows:

> No member shall knowingly approve or employ any advertising on behalf of its lottery or any of its products which is false, misleading or otherwise deceptive as a means of encouraging the purchase of any lottery ticket or service. This rule shall apply to both words and graphic illustrations.
>
> Greed or avarice may not be suggested as a reason to participate in lottery games or services.
>
> No member shall unduly exhort the public to bet by engaging in advertising or other promotional activities which misrepresent by any means, directly or indirectly, a lottery participant's chances of winning any prize, or which denigrate people who do not buy lottery tickets or unduly praise people who do buy tickets. It shall be a violation of this rule to use unqualified or inaccurate language regarding a potential winner's winnings (e.g. "Buy a ticket and be a winner").
>
> Complete and full disclosure of the total prize structure and the odds of winning in each category shall be prominently published and circulated at the outset of all lottery games. The information should appear clearly and con-

spicuously in tabular form in either the initial "launch" advertising created to introduce a game or in the point of purchase brochure or both.[24]

Alan J. Karcher observes, "This code is only honored in its continuous breach. It would be more accurate to say that it is simply ignored."[25] The advertising code may have been adopted with the best of intentions in 1975, but its values are perhaps anachronistic in light of contemporary economic necessities. Reflecting on the nature of lottery advertising, Howard P. Rawlings, a Maryland state legislator, notes:

> Actually, there is a great deal of seduction because of the advertising and promotion. It is done with a keen awareness of human nature. But because it is such an important part of the state revenue structure, no legislator would vote to replace the lottery through the imposition of higher taxes.[26]

Deceptive Promotion

State lotteries also have been charged with deceptive promotional practices. For example, many states do not require that lottery advertisements disclose the chances of winning, especially in the case of huge Lotto jackpots where typical odds are one in five million. The odds of winning the 1998 Powerball jackpot of $195 million climbed to an infinitesimal one in eighty million.[27] The average person is at least eight times more likely to be struck by lightning than to win a lottery jackpot.[28] The Michigan lottery developed a television ad to counter that reasoning. In the commercial, a man asserts resolutely that his chances are better of being struck by lightning than winning the lottery, and then, ZAP, he is hit by a lightning bolt. Scorched, but alive, he says "One ticket, please."[29]

In 1990, fewer than half of the state lotteries disclosed the odds against winning lottery games in print advertising, and only about 25 percent did so in television ads.[30] Not surprisingly, according to the Delaware State Gambling Commission, an average of 92 percent of lottery game players do not know the odds of winning.[31]

Also misleading is the advertised jackpot size. While players are exhorted to try their luck at becoming a millionaire, and images of luxurious, and sometimes fanciful, homes and lifestyles are used to entice participation, few Lotto winners exchange their tickets for multimillion dollar checks. Rather, Lotto jackpots are paid out in twenty yearly installments. The states, not the winners, are able to invest the jackpot funds and collect the interest. This misunderstanding proved to have fatal consequences for one Lotto winner. When Bud Fishman, a computer technician, won $2 million in the Georgia state lottery, he bought a Cape Cod-style house, a Corvette, and a ten-screen multimedia computer entertainment system and received twenty-three pre-approved credit card applications. During a spending spree he maxed out nine new credit cards to finance a new swimming pool. However, when his first annual lottery check of $70,000 arrived, he had to be hospitalized for an anxiety attack. Fishman struggled for three years trying to recover from his tremendous debt before committing suicide by jumping from the roof of his new home.[32]

When some winners realize that the jackpot is paid over the course of twenty years, they take the option of receiving their prize in a one-time, lump-sum payment, but the amount is appreciably smaller than the original jackpot. In either case the winner receives only about 55 *percent* of the prize after federal, state, and local taxes are deducted. Interestingly, state governments require much more stringent payout standards for other forms of gambling than they do for their own lotteries. By law, other forms of legalized gambling must return 80 to 90 percent of gambling funds in prizes. For example, state governments mandate, on average, a payout of 80 percent for pari-mutuel wagering on horses.[33] By comparison, lotteries return only about 50 percent of gambled funds in prizes, representing a relatively poor bet for those who wager.

These troubling questions about the appropriateness of state lotteries as a source of public revenue, and the possible deceptiveness on the part of the state governments in running these lotteries, are compounded by concerns about the relationship between state lotteries and crime. In the 1960s and 1970s, lottery proponents maintained that the absence of state lotteries primarily benefitted organized crime, which controlled the illegal numbers games. However, there is evidence that state lotteries in fact may have increased participation in illegal numbers games.[34] According to *Gaming and Wagering Magazine*, gross revenues for illegal numbers games grew 25 percent between 1982 and 1988.[35] In some states, illegal numbers games operators are taking bets on the state's daily numbers games.[36]

There is also evidence that state lotteries may influence crimes against property. A 1990 study of the fifty states and the District of Columbia from 1970 to 1984 found that the presence of a state lottery was associated with a higher level of property crimes.[37] When other social and economic indicators were controlled, states with lotteries had a rate of property crimes about 3 percent higher than states without, a statistically significant finding. The authors of the study suggested several theories to explain their findings, including the possibility that state lotteries foster a taste in some people for risk-taking activities. They also suggested that the widespread publicity about those who strike it rich in the lottery may increase the feeling of relative deprivation among a segment of the state's population. Earlier research has noted a correlation between relative deprivation and crime.[38]

The states have paid careful attention to protecting their lotteries from the fraud and corruption that contributed to the abolition of lotteries in the late nineteenth century. The first state to establish a contemporary lottery, New Hampshire, was so concerned with the potential for abuse that its first lottery director was a former FBI official. Despite efforts to keep state lotteries beyond reproach, however, there have been instances and allegations of fraud and corruption. One of the most highly publicized incidents occurred in 1981 in Pennsylvania, where all the ping-pong balls used to select the winning numbers, except numbers four and six, were injected with liquid so that they would be heavier and less likely to be selected. However, the individuals involved in the scheme, including the announcer on the broadcast of the lottery numbers selection, were exposed. In 1988 an employee of a lottery supplier printed a ticket with a winning number after the number had already been announced. This scheme, involving a jackpot of $15 million, was also uncovered.

Other allegations concern the awarding of state contracts to lottery suppliers and advertising agencies. For example, in 1994 the world's largest supplier of lottery equipment and lottery operator, GTECH, faced allegations of influence peddling and infringement on business rights. GTECH was investigated by state law enforcement officials in Kentucky and by federal agents in New Jersey.[39] In 1998 GTECH was investigated by British officials for allegations of bribery. It is asserted that GTECH tried to bribe a British tycoon to back off from an offer to run the British National Lottery on a non-profit basis.[40]

Funds for Education: Robbing Peter to Pay Paul

Over the years, the issues surrounding the fairness of state lotteries as a method of taxation have been eclipsed by the rallying cry of many lottery proponents, "more funds for education." The practice of promoting state lotteries with the promise of increased resources for

Table 3.2 Lottery sales and profits earmarking by U.S. state for FY 1996

Lottery	Sales (*million $*)	% profit	Lottery profits earmarking
Arizona	258.8	32	Transportation
			General Fund
			County Assistance
			Economic Development
			Heritage Fund
California	2,295.5	36	Education
Colorado	331.4	29	Parks
			Recreation
			Wildlife
			Open Space
			Public Buildings
Connecticut	706.9	37	General Fund
Delaware	188.5	38	General Fund
D.C.	214.5	37	City's General Fund
Florida	2,117.1	39	Educational Enhancement
			Trust Fund
Georgia	1,592	36	Education
Idaho	92.2	21	Education
			State Building Fund
Illinois	1,634.4	37	Education
Indiana	621.3	30	Education
			Police/Firefighter Pensions
Iowa	190.9	28	General Fund
Kansas	185.0	31	Economic Development
			Prisons
Kentucky	537.7	28	General Fund
Louisiana	291.1	36	General Fund
Maine	148.5	27	General Fund
Maryland	1,113.4	37	General Fund
			Maryland Stadium Authority
Massachusetts	3,028.0	23	Revenue Sharing (Cities and Towns)
Michigan	1,437.8	39	Education
Minnesota	375.7	25	Environment and Natural
			Resources Fund
			General Fund
Missouri	422.5	31	Education
Montana	31,8	26	Education
			Juvenile Detention Centers
Nebraska	81.8	31	Education Innovation Fund
			Environmental Trust Fund
			Landfill Enclosure Fund
New Hampshire	162.9	31	Education
New Jersey	1,587.8	41	Education
			State Institutions

(Table 3.2 continued)

Lottery	Sales (*million $*)	% profit	Lottery profits earmarking
New Mexico	28.0	24	Education (Capital Improvements and Tuition Assistance)
New York	3,610.6	41	Education
Ohio	2,379.5	30	Education
Oregon	689.8	39	Economic Development Education
Pennsylvania	1,673.7	40	Senior Citizens Programs
Rhode Island	455.2	23	General Fund
South Dakota	205.3	35	General Fund Capital Construction Fund
Texas	3,442.7	33	General Fund
Vermont	74.5	30	General Fund
Virginia	924.3	35	General Fund
Washington	389.9	33	General Fund
West Virginia	210.3	31	Education Senior Citizens Parks and Tourism
Wisconsin	482.1	32	Property Tax Relief
Total	34,213.4		

Several states allocate a small portion of proceeds to assist compulsive gamblers, ranging from 1 percent in Nebraska to 0.3 percent in Minnesota.

Sources: Peter Keating, "Lotteries Cannot Resolve the State's Fiscal Crisis," in *Legalized Gambling: For and Against*, ed. Rod L. Evans and Mark Hance (Chicago: Open Court, 1998), 99–111; La Fleur's Lottery World Online, *State Lottery Statistics: U.S. Lotteries' Government Profits Earmarking*, http://www.lafleurs.com/english/statistics/govt.htm (1998).

education prompted H. Roy Kaplan, a sociology professor at the Florida Institute of Technology, to comment:

> There is something cruelly perverse about states encouraging, even proselytizing, their poorest and least educated citizens to gamble, often for the purpose of generating funds for education.[41]

In reality, only sixteen states give a portion of lottery proceeds to education, and, of those states, only ten channel all proceeds to education.[42] A breakdown of how lottery proceeds are distributed in selected states and the total sales per state are shown in Table 3.2. After prizes and costs, the average state keeps only 32.4 percent of lottery sales as profit.

Lottery proceeds actually make up a growing but still small portion of state tax revenues. In 1991, the average lottery contribution to state revenues was 2.02 percent.[43] In 1995, the average had increased to an estimated 3.32 percent.[44] While some state coffers are minimally affected by lottery revenues—Montana revenues were boosted by only 0.9 percent in 1995—other states, such as South Dakota and Oregon, see more substantial contributions, 8.6 and 7.2 percent respectively.[45]

State lotteries constitute a relatively small part of state education revenues. In 1991, state lotteries contributed 11.6 percent of education funding in those states earmarking lottery proceeds just for schools.[46] When state allocations for schools are combined with locally created revenues, the average lottery contribution is only about 3.8 percent.[47]

Thus, many suggest that lotteries have not been the boon for education or other designated services that was promised. In many cases, this is because the amount of funds generated for education by the lottery was equalled by a decrease in the amount of general revenue funds that state legislatures allocated to education. For example, when New York's state lottery generated $95 million more than expected in 1985, the amount of general revenue devoted to education was simply cut by that amount.[48] Illinois is another state that reduced traditional financing for education as lottery dollars came in. In 1989, Belleville, Illinois, school superintendent James Smith complained that education funding in Illinois was actually harmed by the lottery. Not only did the legislature reduce general revenue allocations to schools as the lottery grew, but local officials would not authorize a school bond issue because they believed the schools were "rolling in lottery money."[49] And in 1990 Bill Honig, California public school superintendent, protested that, "For every $5 the lottery gives to schools, the state takes away $4."[50] According to Florida education lobbyist Mario Batista:

> It's a fiscal shell game. The voters approved the lottery thinking education would get a real boost, but instead the state just budgeted that much less for education. More money came into the state, but there was no net gain for education.[51]

Academic studies have supported anecdotal accounts of the "shell game." Three different case studies, one of Michigan and New York, one of Illinois, and one of Florida, all found that lottery funds tended to replace, rather than supplement, funding for education in those states.[52] Moreover, a 1994 study by Thomas H. Jones and John L. Amalfitano of national educational revenues and expenditures concluded that

Lotteries do contribute millions to elementary and secondary education. This is indisputable. But the lottery funds are used in place of other funding.... If using lotteries for education does not result in significant fiscal enhancement, then lotteries produce no educational benefits. This assumption has important implications for educational policy. The gamble that lotteries actually improve America's public schools or their funding is a gamble we can say is already lost.[53]

Finally, a 1995 study by Charles J. Spindler of seven states that earmark lottery proceeds solely for education found that, in most instances, the introduction of a lottery in these states saw a steady increase in education spending for the first few years, only to be followed by "an abrupt decline."[54] So, while lottery sales continue to grow nationally (from $16 billion in 1988 to almost $36 billion in 1997), state lotteries have done relatively little to improve the nation's educational system. Reflecting on the reason for this failure, Charles Spindler writes:

> Despite the earmarking of net lottery revenues, there is no guarantee that state legislatures will not substitute lottery revenues for general education funding. It will be difficult to remedy this lack of accountability for several reasons. First, no state has committed to maintaining a constant ratio of education expenditures to general revenues following the adoption of a lottery. Second, other state agencies will fight for access to new revenues, despite earmarking. Finally, the public is not given complete information regarding education spending.... The lottery can be sold as a means to increase funding for education, while lottery revenues substitute for general fund expenditures. In states where earmarked lottery revenues are used to offset state expenditures for education, the lottery is robbing Peter to pay Paul.[55]

In fact, lotteries ultimately hurt educational financing. Efforts to pass school levies and bond issues in several states have been hampered after a state lottery was adopted because the public believes education is already adequately funded.[56] Moreover, compared to other methods of taxation, lotteries are a "fickle form of finance" because of wide fluctuations in lottery participation. For example, in 1996 nine states and the District of Columbia saw declines in lottery revenues from the previous year.[57] As a result, school administrators are uncertain how much revenue state lotteries will provide from one year to the next. In the words of two lottery critics, "Clearly, a state cannot rely on its lottery to be a stable, reliable source of new revenue. Lottery revenue is affected by changing consumer preferences."[58] In the face of such instability, states respond in the only way they can—through the aggressive promotion of lottery products.

Lotteries and Gambling

While some lottery critics point to the persuasive power of lottery ads, misrepresentations, and crime-related issues, others express concern over the possibility that state lotteries could be promoting gambling, including compulsive gambling. There is some evidence that significant numbers of new gamblers are being drawn from the nation's youth. A study of high-school students in Southern California found that the proportion of those who participated in any form of gambling increased by 40 percent after the state lottery was introduced in 1985.[59] A 1990 study by the Director of the Center for Adolescent Substance Abuse at the University of Minnesota suggests that "gambling-related problems are overtaking drug addiction as the most prevalent problem among teenagers."[60] Results from a sample of 1,094 Minnesota teenagers revealed that 90 percent reported gambling at least once in their lifetime, 20 percent were viewed as "at risk" of becoming compulsive gamblers, and 6 percent were defined as problem gamblers. This research also found that 72 percent of the problem gamblers were regular drug users, compared to 31 percent of those not identified as problem gamblers.[61]

The University of Minnesota study looked at youth gambling in general; a recent study by researchers at the Harvard Medical School, meanwhile, focused on the prevalence of lottery use among children and adolescents in Massachusetts enrolled in grades 7–12.[62] Their examination of a sample of 2,127 students representing ninety-seven Massachusetts public schools revealed that 47 percent of fifth-grade students had purchased lottery tickets at least once, and this proportion increased with age. Among high school seniors, 75 percent had purchased a lottery ticket. Although it is illegal for minors to purchase lottery tickets, 23 percent of the seventh graders reported buying a lottery ticket illicitly during the past thirty days, as did 35 percent of the high-school seniors. The researchers noted:

> Overall, 7.5 percent of Massachusetts youth under the age of 17 purchase at least one lottery ticket every week; 2.7 percent of these young people report buying 20 or more lottery tickets during the past month.[63]

And they warned:

> As access to lottery games and other forms of legal gambling proliferates and receives (1) implicit endorsement (i.e., legal status with no prevention or educational programs) and (2) explicit encouragement (e.g., state-sponsored advertising

and occasional lottery promotional coupons mailed to homes), it is reasonable to expect that gambling among young people will continue to increase.[64]

Linda Berman and Mary-Ellen Siegel, both psychotherapists who work with compulsive gamblers, maintain that state lotteries and easier access to gambling have contributed to an increase in the numbers of gamblers who gamble too much. They maintain that there were "four times as many problem gamblers in 1991 than there were in 1975, and the number continues to grow."[65] Arnold Wexler of the National Council on Compulsive Gambling complains that, due to state lotteries, we are "breeding a society of gamblers—and some of them are going to be compulsive gamblers."[66] It is estimated that 110 million people in the United States now gamble, and as many as five million gamble compulsively.[67] Similarly, one year after the National Lottery was instituted in the U.K., David Alton, a Member of Parliament from Liverpool, noted that "there has been a 17.5 percent increase in calls to Gamblers Anonymous since the lottery began."[68] A 1998 study found that 5 percent of children in the U.K. were compulsive gamblers. Twelve percent of the "problem gamblers" had stolen money from their families to purchase lottery scratch cards, and 15 percent had used lunch or dinner money for such purchases.[69] While quantitative research on the relationship between lotteries and compulsive gambling is not yet available, anecdotal information about the addictive effects of lotteries abounds. Recall from Chapter 1, for example, Tom and Philomena Drake, who gambled their $14,000 savings; Richard Clary, the Florida business executive who embezzled $500,000 to support a $5,000-a-week lottery habit; and Richard Smith, the nineteen-year-old who attempted suicide after spending his savings buying six thousand one-dollar lottery tickets.

Concerned with the possible addictive effects of lotteries, several states, including Nebraska, New York, and Iowa, allocate a small portion of lottery revenues to assist compulsive gamblers. Iowa established a Gamblers' Assistance Fund to support treatment centers throughout the state. Programs such as this, however, individualize the problem by holding gamblers responsible for their own "disorder." The state lottery and the millions of dollars spent on lottery promotion are considered benign. Most other states appear largely untroubled by potential, or existing, problems related to the widespread promotion of lottery gambling, despite the charge by lottery critics that the state has become a *pusher*.[70] New York Times columnist William Safire has observed:

Immoral means have never led to moral ends. We are no longer skimming the profits from a criminal activity: We are putting the full force of government into the promotion of moral corruption.... It is wrong for the state to exploit the weakness of its citizens.[71]

The regressivity of state lotteries and the promotion of gambling, particularly among young people, raise serious questions about the appropriateness of state lotteries. Another issue to consider is whether any special interests are served by the proliferation of state lotteries, and whether these interests exerted undue influence over state governments and the public to institute lotteries.

Although the majority of people may support the creation of state lotteries, lottery initiatives are rarely the result of grassroots organizations. Most lottery referenda are promoted by state legislators and the lottery industry. Lawmakers are looking for revenue without increasing conventional taxes, and the lottery industry is looking for profit. In the mid-1980s Scientific Games, Inc., one of the largest lottery suppliers in the United States, directed pro-lottery ads to officials in states without lotteries. The headline read, "Is Your State Losing Its Share of $3,200,000,000?"[72] The text of the ad stated: "Scientific Games will be pleased to provide state officials with detailed information, revenue projections, expert testimony, and model legislative bills for state operated lotteries."[73] In California, Scientific Games spent $2 million on a lobbying and public relations campaign to get a lottery initiative on the ballot. When the lottery passed with 58 percent of the vote, the company was awarded a $20 million contract to manufacture lottery tickets.[74]

The lottery industry has funded groups such as Californians for Better Education, Citizens for Economic Recovery, and Arizonians for Tax Reduction in states where it has pressed for lottery creation. In the words of Daniel Bower, President of Scientific Games: "Because the establishment of state lotteries is so important to our growth, we actively support any efforts in that regard."[75] The industry's goal was to establish lotteries in forty-seven states by the year 2000.[76]

Pro-lottery coalitions have also received substantial financial support from retail stores hoping to profit from lottery sales. One of the most active has been Southland Corporation, owner of the 7–Eleven convenience stores.

State lotteries have even coordinated their efforts to change or remove any federal laws that hamper lottery-related activities. One of the primary goals of the North American Association of State and Provincial

Lotteries (NASPL), an association representing all the government-authorized lotteries in North America, is

> To coordinate efforts to amend the federal statutes regulating state and provincial lottery jurisdictions, which unnecessarily restrict the ability of state and provincial lottery jurisdictions to operate and serve the public in an efficient manner.[77]

The State

This review of state lotteries as a form of public policy suggests that they are a regressive form of taxation, involve deceptiveness, and promote questionable social behavior. If, as many would argue, lotteries are not in the public interest, why did thirty-seven state governments and the District of Columbia create them, and why do they promote them so aggressively? To answer these questions, one must look at the actions of *state governments* in the broader context of a more general conception of the *state*, of which state governments are one component.

According to the classical sociologist Max Weber, the state is the social institution in a society that holds supreme power and that claims a "monopoly of the legitimate use of force within a given territory."[78] The power of the state is organized through bureaucracies and carried out by government officials. Broadly conceptualized, the modern state is made up of legislative bodies (federal and local), administrations (federal and local), the judiciary, and the military, police, and security forces.

Philosophers and writers have long promoted views of what is proper and desirable conduct by the state. The seventeenth-century philosopher John Locke believed that state power was essentially a public trust that should be used only for the public good. In the eighteenth century, Jean-Jacques Rousseau maintained that only through state-implemented moral restraints could genuine liberty be achieved. These views of the role of the state as advancing moral behavior and promoting the public good are consistent with the writings of Émile Durkheim, the eminent sociologist who wrote during the late nineteenth and early twentieth centuries. Durkheim was very concerned with the potential for modern societies to fall into disorganization and disorder due to their lack of moral cohesion. In the words of sociologist Anthony Giddens, Durkheim believed that

> The characteristic problem facing the modern age is to reconcile the individual freedoms which have sprung from the dissolution of traditional society with the maintenance of the moral control upon which the very existence of society

depends.... [T]he state must play a moral as well as an economic role; and the alleviation of the *malaise* of the modern world must be sought in measures which are in general moral rather than economic.[79]

The nineteenth-century writer Alexis de Tocqueville believed that one of the moral values to be promoted by the state was the importance of building success on hard work. In his famous book *Democracy in America*, de Tocqueville maintained that governments

> must practically teach the community day by day that wealth, fame and power are the rewards of labor, that great success stands at the utmost range of long desires, and that there is nothing lasting but what is obtained by toil.[80]

Despite the visions of the moral good the state should do, many would suggest that the state actually performs a much different role.

A Critical View of the State

For most people, education about the state has been of the "how a bill becomes a law" type, describing the formal organization of the system but rarely addressing the matters of economics and power underlying political structures and decision-making. A critical examination of the state focuses on these elements.

Karl Marx asserted in 1846 that "the State is the form in which the individuals of the ruling class assert their common interests."[81] In essence, Marx viewed the state as a powerful component of the superstructure, one that promulgated laws and values that served the interests of the controllers of wealth. Restating this position in 1884, Friedrich Engels stressed that the state was created as a structural means to promote and protect the appropriation of surplus wealth by a ruling class. Engels asserted that, as egalitarian systems gave way, and in order for the few to exploit the many, a new form of institution was needed,

> an institution which not only served the newly acquired riches of individuals against the communistic traditions ... which not only sanctified the private property formerly so little valued and declared this sanctification to be the highest purpose of all human society; but an institution which set the seal of general social recognition on each new method of acquiring property and thus amassing wealth at continually increasing speed; an institution which perpetuated not only this growing cleavage of society into classes but also the right of the possessing class to exploit the non-possessing, and the rule of the former over the latter.

And this institution came. The *state* was invented.[82]

From this perspective, the primary purpose of the state is to preserve a system of oppression and the resulting maldistribution of wealth. As Weber noted, the state holds a monopoly on the legitimate use of force; Marxists would add that such force frequently has been applied against those who threaten the interests of the ruling class. There are innumerable historical examples of such use of force within the United States.[83]

There are other ways besides force through which the state can protect and enhance the interests of the ruling class. Indeed, constant and mass use of violence to control the members of a society is time-consuming and expensive and may well lead to plots and rebellions. Instead, the ruling class may obtain general acceptance of its power and privileges by promulgating ideas that legitimate them. That is to say, the interests of the ruling class must come to be viewed as being the same as, and actually promoting, the public interest. Writing in 1844, Marx observed that a dominant class must

> arouse, in itself and in the masses, a moment of enthusiasm in which it associates and mingles with society at large, identifies with it, and is felt and recognized as the *general representative* of this society.[84]

Marx and Engels believed that, in most instances, the ruling class is successful in promulgating its views. They wrote:

> The ideas of the ruling class are in every epoch the ruling ideas, i.e., the class which is the ruling *material* force of society, is at the same time its ruling *intellectual* force.... Insofar, therefore, as they rule as a class and determine the extent and compass of an epoch, it is self-evident that they do this in its whole range, hence among other things rule also as thinkers, as producers of ideas, and regulate the production and distribution of the ideas and their age: thus their ideas are the ruling ideas of the epoch.[85]

From this point of view, the state is key in promoting the ideas, and thus the interests, of the ruling class. However, efficient states must exercise some finesse so as to package their actions as reflecting the "public interest."

Due to current ideological forces, many will argue that such an analysis of the state is no longer relevant, especially for the contemporary United States. From this point of view, the contemporary state is now essentially democratic, and old forms of rule by the elite have been largely exorcised from existing procedures, laws, and policies. Some writers, like political scientist Robert A. Dahl, contend that in the contemporary United States political power is dispersed among a wide variety of interest groups and that no single powerful group exerts substantial influence over state policy.[86]

Twentieth-century Marxist theorists contend that this perspective, commonly referred to as *pluralism*, obscures the influence that the wealthy and powerful continue to exercise over the state. Among neo-Marxists there are two general views on how this control is exercised. Some Marxists characterize the state as an *instrument* used by the dominant economic class on a daily basis to maintain their control over social arrangements. For example, sociologist G. William Domhoff has documented that members of the upper class are overrepresented in powerful corporate and government positions. He writes:

> [The] owners and top-level managers in large income-producing properties are far and away the dominant figures in the United States. Their corporations, banks, and agribusiness come together as a corporate community that dominates the federal government in Washington.[87]

Neo-Marxist scholar Ralph Miliband points to the powerful, yet frequently indiscernible, influence the economically powerful can exert over the state.[88] Highly aware of the enormous concentration of economic power that characterizes twentieth-century capitalism, and of the fact that economic elites control important sectors of the economy, Miliband suggests that the economically dominant class continues to promote its interests through the very democratic institutions that ostensibly were created to thwart rule by the few. Miliband believes that this influence is exercised in various ways. First, citizens are *indoctrinated* to accept the values and organization of capitalist society. Americans are taught that capitalism is more or less synonymous with patriotism. Miliband suggests that, although the system of education in the United States cannot easily be charged with brainwashing, educators can hardly avoid presenting information that is highly supportive of the prevailing social and political order. We are taught that to criticize capitalism is to be a "Red" or a "Commie" and is a threat to the "American way of life."

Some would dispute this position by arguing that indoctrination cannot occur in a country where people are free to offer opposing views and ideas. However, Miliband states that,

> For indoctrination to occur, it is not necessary that there should be monopolistic control and the prohibition of opposition; it is only necessary that ideological competition be so unequal as to give a crushing advantage to one side or the other.[89]

Miliband further suggests that in capitalist societies certain political parties are "the favored, chosen vehicles or instruments of the business classes and of the dominant classes generally."[90] While membership in these parties may be broad-based, the leadership is composed largely of people from the upper and middle classes. These parties are particularly attentive to the concerns of the dominant classes, who provide them with considerable financial support—a point of no small magnitude in the democracies of capitalist societies. Miliband maintains that these conservative political parties tend to receive a significant degree of direct, and indirect, support from churches, and are further sustained by strong sentiments of *nationalism*. Miliband writes that, in the exploitation of national sentiments,

> conservative parties are powerfully helped by innumerable agencies of civil society which are, to a greater or lesser degree, involved in the propagation of a "national" view and of a "national interest" defined in conservative terms.[91]

Moreover, Miliband contends that big business not only exerts tremendous control over political parties and the definition of the national interest but also has the resources to promote directly a public acceptance of the ethos, values, and goals of business through their "abundant expression in every kind of medium."[92] Miliband charges that the mass media in capitalist society are "both the expression of a system of domination, and a means of reinforcing it."[93] The assumed impartiality and objectivity of the mass media are largely illusory, and the preponderance of information stemming from the mass media supports the status quo, because the dominant economic classes exert substantive control through ownership of the media and through paid advertising. Thus, Miliband concludes, the tremendous economic and social power that is held in the hands of the economically dominant classes permits them to enjoy a "massive preponderance in society, in the political system, and in the determination of the state's policies and actions."[94] Miliband finds that

> the state ... is primarily and inevitably the guardian and protector of the economic interests which are dominant in them. Its "real" purpose and mission is to ensure their continued predominance, not to prevent it.[95]

While some scholars view the state as an *instrument* of a class-conscious ruling class, others picture the state as a relatively autonomous *structure* that supports private property and capitalism. That is, the state was designed and structured to insulate powerful interests from any substantial popular democratic efforts to create a more equitable society.[96] From this perspective, the state in capitalist societies, and especially the United States, has been transformed so that it is no longer merely a mechanism of ruling-class control but instead plays a central role in the protection and maintenance of capitalism. Instead of seeing the state as controlled by a relatively small number of economically powerful people, structuralists see the state as inherently designed to control conflict among powerful elites while regulating the economy for the good of the entire capitalist order.

One version of the structuralist position was developed by James O'Connor.[97] According to O'Connor, the modern capitalist state performs two basic functions: capital accumulation and system legitimation. The state must try to create and maintain conditions that are conducive to private, profitable capital accumulation and at the same time legitimate class society and keep the peace. Some state policies and expenditures are made to maintain and increase profitable productivity, while others are made to reduce dissent and facilitate social harmony. O'Connor suggests, however, that these two contradictory goals, of creating both profitable capital and social harmony, are fundamentally incompatible and crisis-inducing. This is true because, while the state spreads the cost of profitable capital accumulation among the entire citizenry, the comparatively few beneficiaries of this process resist taxation, limiting the resources available to fund the continually increasing costs of public and human services.

This brief excursion into theoretical examinations of the state helps to answer the question posed earlier: why did state governments create lotteries in the latter part of the twentieth century, when such a program is unfair and harmful to the public? If the polished public image of the state (not individual politicians) is examined with an eye to political-economic-social history, the superficial shine is quickly tarnished. A critical interpretation of the role of the state in capitalist society resonates with truth, particularly when the lives and history of those who were and are poor or devalued are considered.[98]

While economic forces played a considerable role in the reemergence of state lotteries, the state has embraced and legitimated their return. This public policy is best understood as a combination of the state's tendencies to protect wealth, to indoctrinate the public to accept economic disparities, and to respond to the late-twentieth-century crisis of public finance—as opposed to simply benignly promoting lotteries in order to "fund good schools for kids." Critical theory also helps to explain why and how the state acted to deepen the public funding crisis of late-twentieth-century capitalism, thus paving the way for Lottomania.

The next section will review some of the actions of the federal and state governments that contributed to the need for, and the creation of, state lotteries.

The State as Protector of Capitalists and Capitalism

As maintained in the previous chapter, although dramatic disparities in wealth and income existed in the United States during the boom years of the 1950s and 1960s, the economic problems that prompted the widespread adoption of state lotteries grew in the 1970s. Economic concentration continued, and corporations had become a powerful component of the means of production and one of the primary ways in which the dominant economic class maintained and exercised control. By 1972 the wealthiest 1 percent of the population of the U.S. owned 56.5 percent of all privately held corporate stock, and the wealthiest one-half percent held 49.3 percent of such stock.[99] By the mid-twentieth century the interests of the dominant economic class and large corporations had become congruent. So it is not surprising that when U.S. corporations were threatened by growing global economic competition and increasing energy costs the federal government acted to support the corporations and, thus, the interests of the dominant economic class. In so doing, however, the government actually provided incentives for the process of deindustrialization and corporate relocations and contributed to the fiscal crisis that began the wave of state lotteries in the 1970s and 1980s.

A variety of federal government actions and policies promoted the interests of the economically powerful but hurt the public, either directly or indirectly. One example was the attempt by the federal government to boost domestic oil production during the "oil crisis" of the late 1970s. When the petroleum-producing nations of the Middle East joined together to take control of oil prices, U.S. oil companies lobbied the government to remove price controls so they would have more funds to search for new sources of oil. However, the arguments of the oil companies in favor of removing price controls were contradicted by the tremendous amounts of capital they were using to acquire other businesses, often unrelated to the energy industry. For example, during this period Standard Oil used its excess capital to purchase

Kennecott Corporation, the nation's leading producer of copper. Exxon acquired Reliance Electric Company, the nation's third largest manufacturer of electric motors, paying Reliance's stockholders more than 200 percent of the prevailing market value of their stock.[100] Mobil lost a takeover fight with Dupont and Seagrams for Conoco, Inc., but successfully obtained Montgomery Ward. Despite such uses of excess capital, President Carter decontrolled oil prices in 1979.

Another benefit for corporations, the virtually unlimited deductibility of the interest on corporate debt, fueled the use of high-yield junk bonds, widely used in financing corporate mergers and acquisitions. More than four thousand such deals, worth $190 billion, took place in 1986 alone.[101] In many instances, companies were acquired only so that their assets could be sold off, a practice that was very profitable to owners, investors, and corporate executives but that often resulted in closed factories and lost jobs. When pressure was brought on Congress to scale back the almost unlimited tax breaks on corporate debt interest, a group of powerful financiers formed an organization called the Alliance for Capital Access, whose sole purpose was to block any federal restraint on junk bonds. The Alliance effectively stopped any changes in the tax laws that would scale back deductions on corporate debt interest, spending $4.9 million between 1985 and 1990 on lobbying efforts.[102] Their expenses included lunches, banquets, floral arrangements, gifts, and limousine services for members of Congress and their staffs.

While federal policy facilitated greater economic concentration by promoting acquisitions, it also fueled the movement of plants and jobs to low-wage areas—many outside the country—by preferential tax and tariff treatment of foreign investment. According to Barry Bluestone and Bennett Harrison, although federal policy was not the *cause* of the shifting of corporations investments overseas,

> public policies reinforced corporate decisions that were based on more important factors: markets, labor costs, and political security. But this is no trivial point. It implies that managers who invested abroad were rewarded with windfall profits from the IRS.... For example, the U.S. Tax Code was rewritten to permit American corporations to credit all of their foreign income taxes against their domestic tax liabilities on a dollar for dollar basis. This constitutes a far greater saving than is normally available on other business expenses, which are usually deducted from the revenue at the taxable "bottom line."[103]

Moreover, another incentive for foreign investments was a policy permitting U.S. corporations to defer the payment of taxes to the nation until profits are actually repatriated; in many instances, corporations are able to put off repatriations indefinitely.[104] In addition to tax benefits, special federal programs were created to directly subsidize foreign investment. One of these federal programs, the U.S. Export–Import Bank,

> used $310 million of taxpayer money to finance the transfer by Dow Chemical, Ford, Alcoa, Goodyear, B.F. Goodrich, Armco Steel, Kaiser, Reynolds, and Union Carbide of $410 million worth of equipment from their American plants to various subsidiaries in the Third World.[105]

The U.S. tariff system provided further incentive for foreign investment. Basic components of computer chips, automobiles, aircraft parts, textiles, clothing, televisions, radios, and numerous other products can be manufactured in the U.S., shipped to a third world country for assembly, and then shipped back to the U.S. for sale. A duty is paid only on the value added in the foreign assembly process, not on the market value of the finished product. This policy encouraged the phenomenon known as "runaway shops," and contributed to the proliferation of *maquilladoras*, or border assembly plants, in a tax-free, tariff-free zone created by Mexico just across the U.S.–Mexico border. Numerous U.S. corporations, including North American Rockwell, Burroughs, General Instrument, GTE Sylvania, RCA, Levi Strauss, Puritan and Kayser-Roth, Motorola, Hughes Aircraft, General Motors, and Chrysler, have transferred work to or opened plants in Mexico.[106] These U.S. corporations pay low-wage Mexican laborers, primarily women, to assemble their products, which are then shipped back to the U.S. with duty paid only on the value added—that is, the cost of the cheap Mexican labor.

By way of another example, in 1976 the tax code was amended to provide tax credits for U.S. corporations that established subsidiaries in Puerto Rico; the companies in the United States could receive the profits of these subsidiaries without paying corporate income taxes. Corporations could both avoid taxes and increase their profits by paying the lower wages of Puerto Rican workers. Meanwhile, across the country, working people lost jobs and state and local governments lost tax revenues. One worker who lost his job when his employer moved its operations from Elkhart, Indiana, to Puerto Rico was George Skelton, who worked for American Home Products, manufacturer of such products as Advil, Anacin, Preparation H, and Dristan. Skelton's case was cited in the 1992 book *America: What Went Wrong?* by Pulitzer

Prize-winning investigative reporters Donald L. Barlett and James B. Steele. Barlett and Steele write:

> George Skelton's loss—the loss of other Elkhart workers—is American Home Products' gain. Listen to the words of Smith Barney, Harris Upham and Company, a Wall Street investment firm that reported in April 1990 on the good tax-fortunes of American Home Products: "In 1985, American Home Products initiated tax-sheltered manufacturing in Puerto Rico.... As a result, American Home Products' tax rate declined 13.9 percentage points from 1983 to 1988." ... Said the fifty-two-year-old Skelton: "All the companies that have moved down there, so far as I know, are good, healthy, rich companies. It's like giving welfare to the rich, the way I'm looking at it. Robbing from the poor and giving it to the rich."[107]

Another federal policy ostensibly intended to promote economic growth and the ability of business to respond better to global economic competition was deregulation, or reduced government control of business activities. Efforts toward deregulation began during the Carter administration and came to fruition during the Reagan years. Deregulation of a number of industries, including transportation, telecommunications, financial services, and oil, was promoted as serving both consumers and the economy. Reflecting on some of the effects of the deregulation wave that peaked in the mid-1980s, Kevin Phillips writes:

> By mid-decade, however, some doubts were developing. The first involved safety—deregulation's contribution to reckless financial speculation, marginal airline maintenance practices, bank failures, truck highway accidents and corporate sacrifice of long-term goals to deal with raiders. The second concerned fairness. Deregulation helped some groups and regions and hurt others.... Prosperous individuals and financial institutions *were* the most obvious beneficiaries.[108]

One of the most dramatic economic effects of deregulation was the collapse of the savings and loan industry. Due in large part to greed and fraud, this economic catastrophe is costing the nation an estimated $500 billion.

Finally, income tax cuts orchestrated by the Reagan administration gave substantial income tax breaks to corporations and affluent individuals. These policies were ostensibly to spur new investment and growth. In reality, however, much of the capital generated by these tax cuts was instead placed in safe, and often *unproductive*, investments and activities that did little to create jobs or provide economic expansion. Personal income tax rates for those in the top bracket dropped from 70 percent to 28 percent between 1980 and 1987.[109] By 1983 federal tax receipts from corporate income taxes dropped to an all-time low of 6.2 percent, down from 12.5 percent in 1980 and 32.1 percent in 1952.[110] Further, the top rate for taxes on capital gains was reduced to 20 percent, down 29 percentage points since 1978.[111]

This sample of federal policies, in conjunction with massive cuts in federal spending on social programs, proved to be a bonanza for the affluent but a disaster for millions of working and economically marginalized citizens. Between 1977 and 1989, 60 percent of newly created income in the United States went to the wealthiest 1 percent of the nation's families.[112] According to Barlett and Steele, the United States government has "rigged" the economy to favor the rich.

> [T]hose people in Washington who write the complex tangle of rules by which the economy operates have, over the past twenty years, rigged the game—by design and default—to favor the privileged, the powerful and the influential. At the expense of everyone else....
>
> As a result, the already rich are richer than ever; there has been an explosion in overnight new rich; life for the working class is deteriorating, and those at the bottom are trapped. For the first time in this century, members of the generation entering adulthood will find it almost impossible to achieve a better lifestyle than their parents. Most will be unable to even match their parents' middle-class status.[113]

If federal government policies ostensibly adopted to create jobs and strengthen corporate responses to global competition were in reality a boon for the affluent—and created a climate conducive to the re-emergence of lotteries—what about the actions of *state governments*?

Who Controls State Governments?

The United States has a *federal* system of government, meaning that governmental power is shared by a national government and smaller regional governments. Although the national government can make laws with which the individual states must comply, the states maintain a substantial degree of latitude and responsibility in governing. For example, state governments play a significant role in regulating insurance, public utilities, and transportation and in building and maintaining highways; states create most of the criminal laws and try the vast majority of all court cases. They are responsible for the primary and secondary public schools and most of the nation's colleges and universities, administer social services and public welfare programs, operate prisons and institutions for people with disabilities, and carry out a host of other responsibilities. Their importance was noted by a nineteenth-century writer, who maintained that the states relieved the federal government of

> that large mass of functions which might otherwise prove too heavy for it. Thus business is more promptly dispatched and the great central council of the nation has time to deliberate on those qualities which most nearly touch the whole country.[114]

Do state governments, as seen with the federal government, also reflect the interests of the economically powerful? Some observers maintain that state governments actually may be *more* susceptible to the influence of the affluent than is the federal government. According to political analysts Milton C. Cummings, Jr. and David Wise:

> Public respect for state legislators and legislatures has also been eroded by occasional disclosure of corruption among the lawmakers. Perhaps few state legislators can be "bought" by direct bribes, but there is some feeling among the public that state legislators, one way or another, manage to use their position for private gain. Closely tied to this assumption is the belief that lobbyists and special interest groups can work their will at the statehouse more easily than in Washington.[115]

G. William Domhoff also contends that members of the ruling social class exert considerable influence on state and local politics. He notes that the power elite exercise this influence through campaign finances and lobbying.[116] Money from political action committees (PACs) played an increasing role in state elections and ballot issues during the 1980s, and PAC growth has been "disproportionate among business and professional interests."[117] Some PACs seem to specialize in pouring out-of-state money into local elections; one state reported that 60 percent of funds contributed to local elections came from outside the state.[118] According to sociologist Amitai Etzioni,

> [L]arge nationally based PACs such as BANKPAC and AMPAC [the PAC of the American Medical Association] can give $5,000 to the candidate of their choice. Out-of-state money supports a variety of causes, but some of the largest amounts flow from Southern and Southwestern oil PACs, all conservative, to oppose Northern liberals.[119]

The economically powerful also tend to dominate the very regulatory boards and commissions that were created to protect the public interest. White-collar employees who also hold public office are unlikely to support legislation or policies that go against the interests of their corporate employers. Moreover, the power elite control most mass circulation newspapers, television and radio stations, and they exert considerable control over foundations and charities.[120] Finally, the corporate rich can threaten to—and actually do—move business operations out of an inhospitable state or city.

In their efforts to remain financially solvent during times of de-industrialization and strong anti-taxation sentiments, and to compete successfully with other states to retain and attract business activity, state and local governments have been striving to become more "business-friendly." Most states have offered businesses such relocation incentives as tax abatements and free or reduced rates for infrastructure construction such as access roads and water and sewerage connections. The following is but one example provided by Joe R. Feagin and Robert Parker of the power a large business can exert over a state government:

> In the mid-1980s ConAgra, an Omaha-based food processing conglomerate, began looking for a site for a new research facility and headquarters. ConAgra's chief executive informed Nebraska government officials that his company would consider staying in the state if they would modify the tax laws. He told the governor and the state legislature that these specific changes would be necessary for ConAgra to remain: a reduction in the personal income tax for the high income bracket, a shrinking of the taxable base of corporate earnings to reflect only in-state sales (a major break), a package of investment and payroll tax credits, and property and equipment tax exemptions (including some for Con-Agra's jet airplanes).... ConAgra executives got what they asked for. Originally, it was estimated that the tax breaks would deprive the state treasury of $24 million in the first few years, but a closer examination revealed a loss of at least $160 million.[121]

Yielding further to corporate pressure, some states have restricted labor union activity by passing "right-to-work" legislation.[122] These laws prohibit union contracts from requiring that workers at a unionized job site join the union, making it difficult for labor unions to organize effectively. From the employer's perspective, one of the primary benefits of the "right-to-work" laws is the reduced likelihood that workers will organize to oppose poor wages or benefits or to challenge working conditions.

Many states even try to attract businesses by *advertising* that they offer low wages and a passive labor force. The Florida Department of Commerce boasts in ads to prospective businesses that less than 13 percent of its non-agricultural labor force is unionized and that its "right-to-work" law results in a low level of labor unrest and work stoppages.[123] Texas, Virginia, and Oklahoma all advertise that "wage rates are considerably below those found in major manufacturing areas."[124]

Given such conditions, the need for state lotteries can easily be understood. How else are state governments to fund public and human services? How are millions of people who have lost their jobs and who struggle to find low-paying replacement jobs to channel their frustration and insecurity? A lottery provides a partial answer to both questions.

For state governments, a lottery is one of the only taxes acceptable to the affluent, a regressive tax. Although lotteries were outlawed for decades, states must now vigorously promote them even though they place more of the burden of public finance onto those who can least afford it. And they must largely ignore the possibility, and reality, of increasing crime, compulsive gambling, and gambling among young people. Moreover, many states promote lotteries as benefitting schools and human services when in reality lottery funds largely just replace funds previously allocated from other sources. Many states then withhold information from their citizens—if they do not outright deceive them—about the chances of winning and the actual amount of money to be won.

The state in capitalist society, long a protector of private property and wealth, is capable of immoral and even illegal actions when the system is challenged or the economically powerful are confronted with serious political threats from below. In times of economic crisis, the state has demonstrated a willingness to shift resources to the economically powerful, forcing state governments to adopt and promote a tax that is unfair and arguably promotes undesirable social behavior. These state actions stray considerably from the function of the state envisioned by Locke, Rousseau, and Durkheim. Using the glitzy modern media to exhort their citizens to pursue their dreams through the lottery is a far cry from de Tocqueville's admonition to governments to teach the community "that wealth, fame and power are the rewards of labor," and that "there is nothing lasting but what is obtained by toil."

Looking at the actions of the states and the federal government that have led to the reemergence of lotteries, one can see evidence that supports both of the Marxist theories concerning the role of the state, as an *instrument* and as an *autonomous structure*. For example, the fact that powerful economic interests have exerted considerable control over state decision-making supports the theory that the state is an instrument of the dominant classes. From the Alliance for Capital Access to the increasing numbers of corporate PACs to the powerful lottery industry that spent millions of dollars lobbying state officials and promoting initiative campaigns for the creation of lotteries, there is evidence of direct control of the state by the economically powerful and the corporations they control. While the use of this influence may not be a coordinated or conspiratorial effort on the part of a dominant economic class as a whole, the deliberate and calculated actions by segments of the dominant class frequently serve the general interests of the privileged group as a whole.

On the other hand, structuralists can point to the fact that the state is predictably performing its function to facilitate capital accumulation and profit generation, especially during the period when corporations are adjusting to global competition. Favorable tax and tariff policies, deregulation, direct subsidies to corporations, and laws that undermine organized labor are produced more by the design of the state than by the conscious manipulations of the elite. That is, the state is designed so that only those loyal to the interests of the elite can obtain power, and actions contrary to their interests could cause the present economic order to unravel. So, by design, the state acts to promote profit accumulation. However, a fiscal crisis is intensified as public revenues are ceded, ostensibly to induce public economic growth and production but in reality often serving to promote greater personal enrichment for the few. Correspondingly, entire communities and countless families experience loss of jobs and revenues, frequently with devastating consequences. This crisis was further compounded in the 1980s when drastic cuts were made in housing, education, health care, day care, and other social programs that facilitate social harmony, in order to shift even more resources to support capital accumulation. The resulting fiscal crisis is ameliorated, in a small but significant way, by the development of lotteries. State lotteries, largely independent of the direct influence of economically powerful people, daily exhort the masses of ordinary people to gamble to achieve their dreams. Based on the high level of public participation in lottery games, one could conjecture that, in a time of declining social service programs that legitimate the system and promote harmony, acceptance of vast inequities is braced by the hope of winning a Lotto jackpot.

While contemporary Marxist scholars may debate the degree to which the state is directly and consciously controlled by powerful members of the dominant economic class, all would agree that state actions continue to protect and enhance the interests of that class. Actions by the state, in the form of both state and federal governments, have been the primary impetus for the creation of, and participation in, state lotteries.

Notes

1. Alan J. Karcher, *Lotteries* (New Brunswick, NJ: Transaction Publishers), 38.
2. Charles T. Clotfelter and Philip J. Cook, *Selling Hope: State Lotteries in America* (Cambridge, MA: Harvard University Press, 1989), 216.
3. Cited in "Taxation," Chapter 14 in *The Annals of America: Great Issues in American Life* (A Conspectus), Volume II (Chicago: Encyclopedia Britannica, Inc, 1968), 87.
4. "Lottery is Financed by the Poor and Won by the States," *New York Times*, May 21, 1989, VI, 4: 1.
5. Clotfelter and Cook, *Selling Hope*, 229.
6. Daniel B. Suits, "Gambling as a Source of Revenue," in *Michigan's Fiscal and Economic Structure*, ed. Harvey Brazer and Deborah Laren (Ann Arbor: University of Michigan Press, 1982), 833.
7. Daniel B. Suits, "Gambling Taxes: Regressivity and Revenue Potential," *National Tax Journal*, 30, no. 1 (1977), 19–35.
8. Charles T. Clotfelter, "On the Regressivity of State-Operated 'Numbers' Games," *National Tax Journal*, 32, no. 4 (1979), 543–47.
9. Roger E. Brinner and Charles T. Clotfelter, "An Economic Appraisal of State Lotteries," *National Tax Journal*, 28, no. 4 (December 1975), 395–403; Michael H. Spiro, "On the Tax Incidence of the Pennsylvania Lottery," *National Tax Journal*, 27, no. 1 (March 1974), 57–61; and Frederick D. Stocker, "State Sponsored Gambling as a Source of Public Revenue," *National Tax Journal*, 25, no. 3 (September 1972), 437–41.
10. Gary S. Becker, "Higher Sin Taxes: A Low Blow to the Poor." *Business Week*, June 5, 1989, 23.
11. Daniel J. Brown, Dennis O. Kaldenberg, and Beverly A. Browne, "Socio-Economic Status and Playing the Lotteries," *Sociology and Social Research*, 76, no. 3 (1992), 161–67.
12. Maureen Pirog-Good and John L. Mikesell, "Longitudinal Evidence of the Changing Socio-Economic Profile of a State Lottery Market," *Policy Studies Journal*, 23, no. 3 (1995), 451–65.
13. Ronald Alsop, "State Lottery Craze is Spreading, But Some Fear It Hurts the Poor," *Wall Street Journal*, February 24, 1983; cited in Clotfelter and Cook, *Selling Hope*, 215.
14. Karcher, *Lotteries*, 39.
15. Robert Uhlig, "Hawking Fires a Brief Tirade Against Lottery," *Electronic Telegraph*, February 14, 1996, 1, http://www.telegraph.co.uk.
16. Becker, "Higher Sin Taxes," 23.
17. *Chicago Tribune*, March 13, 1986; cited in Clotfelter and Cook, *Selling Hope*, 229.
18. *Washington Post*, January 26, 1990, C6.
19. Karcher, *Lotteries*, 58.

20. Ibid., 58.
21. *Riverfront Times*, March 14–20, 1990, 9.
22. Clotfelter and Cook, *Selling Hope*, 229; Institute for Policy Research, *Most Ohioans Play Lottery*, Press Release, November 27, 1989, University of Cincinnati.
23. Clotfelter and Cook, *Selling Hope*, 207.
24. Karcher, *Lotteries*, 81–82.
25. Ibid., 82.
26. *Washington Post*, January 14, 1990, C1.
27. P. Solomon Banda, "Millions Taking Shot at $150 Million Jackpot," *Dayton Daily News*, May 19, 1998, 4A.
28. Ibid., 12A.
29. Karcher, *Lotteries*, 83.
30. Ibid., 12.
31. Ibid.
32. Jerry Benson, "Pennies from Hell," *Omni*, 13, no. 9 (June 1991), 112.
33. Ibid.
34. Judith H. Hybels, "The Impact of Legalization on Illegal Gambling Participation," *Journal of Social Issues*, 35 (1979), 27–35.
35. Amy Bayer, "Are Lotteries A Ripoff?" *Consumer's Research*, January 1990, 14.
36. Ibid.
37. John Mikesell and Maureen A. Pirog-Good, "State Lotteries and Crime: The Regressive Revenue is Linked With a Crime Rate Higher by 3 Percent," *American Journal of Economics and Sociology*, 49, no. 1 (1990), 7–18.
38. Ibid., 9.
39. *Dayton Daily News*, March 13, 1994, B1.
40. Dirk Beveridge, The Boston Globe Online: http://www.boston.online/dailynews/wirehtml/203_lr/gtech_spokesman_wins_his_part_of_br.htm (1998).
41. H. Roy Kaplan, "The Social and Economic Impact of State Lotteries," *The Annals of the American Academy of Political and Social Science*, 477, January 1985, 91–106.
42. Those states are California, Florida, Georgia, Illinois, Michigan, Missouri, Montana, New Hampshire, New York, and Ohio.
43. David P. Brandon, *State Run Lotteries: Their Effects on School Funding* (Arlington, VA: Educational Research Service, 1993), 6.
44. Based on analysis of data appearing in Peter Keating's "Lotteries Cannot Resolve the States' Fiscal Crisis," in *Legalized Gambling: For and Against*, ed. Rod L. Evans and Mark Hance (Chicago: Open Court, 1998) 107–10.
45. Ibid.
46. Brandon, *State-Run Lotteries*, 5.
47. Ibid.
48. "Gambling and the State," *The Economist*, April 11, 1992, 24.
49. "The States Like the Odds," *Time*, July 10, 1989, 19.
50. William H. Willimon, "Lottery Losers," *Christian Century*, January 17, 1990, 48.
51. Bayer, "Are Lotteries a Ripoff?" 15.
52. Marsha Jane Stewart, "Patterns of Revenues for Public Elementary and Secondary School Education Derived as a Result of State Lotteries: A Case

Study of Michigan and New York," *Dissertation Abstracts International*, 48, no. 1114A (1987); Mary O. Borg and Paul M. Mason, "Earmarked Lottery Revenues: Positive Windfalls or Concealed Redistribution Mechanisms?" *Journal of Education Finance*, 15, no. 3 (1990), 298–301; Steven D. Stark, D. S. Honeyman, and R. Craig Wood, *An Examination of the Florida Educational Lottery*, Occasional Paper No. 3 (Gainesville, FL: UCEA Center for Educational Finance, Department of Educational Leadership, University of Florida, 1991).

53. Thomas H. Jones and John L. Amalfitano, *America's Gamble: Public School Finance and State Lotteries* (Basel: Technomic Publishing, 1994), 149–50.

54. Charles J. Spindler, "The Lottery and Education: Robbing Peter to Pay Paul?" *Public Budgeting and Finance*, 15, no. 3 (1995), 54–62.

55. Ibid., 60–61.

56. Brandon, *State-Run Lotteries*, 13.

57. International Gaming and Wagering Business, *North American Gaming Report* (New York, 1997).

58. John L. Mikesell and C. Kurt Zorn, "State Lotteries as Fiscal Savior or Fiscal Fraud: A Look at the Evidence," *Public Administration Review*, July/August 1986, 314.

59. "Lotto is Financed by the Poor and Won by the States," *New York Times*, May 21, 1989, IV, 6: 1.

60. Ken C. Winters, "The Odds of Problem Teenage Gambling," *School Intervention Report*, 4, no. 5 (April/May 1991), 2.

61. Ibid., 3.

62. Howard J. Schaffer and Matthew Hall, *The Emergence of Youthful Gambling and Drug Use: The Prevalence of Underage Lottery Use and the Impact of Gambling* (Boston: Harvard Medical School, 1994).

63. Ibid., 10.

64. Ibid., 15–16.

65. Linda Berman and Mary-Ellen Siegel, *Behind the Eight Ball: A Guide for Families of Gamblers* (New York: Simon & Schuster, 1992), 49.

66. Clotfelter and Cook, *Selling Hope*, 124.

67. John J. O'Connor, "The Urge to Gamble, and How to Fight Addiction," *New York Times*, June 29, 1990, C24.

68. George Jones, "Lottery Jackpot Curb is Rejected," *Electronic Telegraph*, October 26, 1995, 1, http://www.telegraph.co.uk.

69. Rachel Sylvester, "Camelot Ordered to Curb the Under-Age Scratchcard Addicts," *Electronic Telegraph*, February 26, 1998, 1, http://www.telegraph.co.uk.

70. "The Economic Case Against State-Run Gambling," *Business Week*, August 4, 1975, 67–68.

71. William Safire, "When States Roll Dice, Poor Must Pay Up," *St. Louis Post–Dispatch*, April 26, 1991, 3C.

72. Karcher, *Lotteries*, 23.

73. Ibid., 23.

74. Bayer, "Are Lotteries a Ripoff?," 12–13.

75. Ibid., 12.

76. Ibid., 13.

77. North American Association of State and Provincial Lotteries, *Lottery Facts and Background Information* (Washington, DC, 1994).

78. Max Weber, *From Max Weber: Essays in Sociology*, ed. H. H. Gerth and C. Wright Mills (New York: Oxford University Press, 1946), 78.

79. Anthony Giddens, *Capitalism and Modern Social Theory: An Analysis of the Writings of Marx, Durkheim and Max Weber* (New York: Cambridge University Press, 1971), 99.

80. Cited in Virgil W. Peterson, "Gambling: Should It Be Legalized?" *Journal of Criminal Law and Criminology*, 40, no. 3 (September/October 1949), 326.

81. Karl Marx, *Karl Marx: Selected Writings in Sociology and Social Philosophy* (New York: McGraw-Hill, 1956 [1846]), 223.

82. Friedrich Engels, *The Origins of the Family, Private Property and the State* (New York: Penguin Books, 1986 [1884]), 141.

83. See, for example, Alan Wolfe's *The Seamy Side of Democracy: Repression in America* (New York: Longman, 1978); and Vincent Pinto's "Soldiers and Strikers: Class Repression as State Policy," in *The Capitalist System*, Second Edition, ed. Richard C. Edwards, Michael Reich and Thomas E. Weisskopf (Englewood Cliffs, NJ: Prentice Hall, 1978).

84. Cited in *Crime and Capitalism: Readings in Marxist Criminology*, ed. David F. Greenberg (Philadelphia: Temple University Press, 1993), 469.

85. Karl Marx and Friedrich Engels, *The German Ideology* (New York: International Publishers, 1989 [1845]), 64–65.

86. Robert A. Dahl, *Who Governs?* (New Haven, CT: Yale University Press, 1961).

87. G. William Domhoff, *Who Rules America?: Power and Politics in the Year 2000*, Third Edition (Mountain View, CA: Mayfield Publishing, 1998), 1.

88. Ralph Miliband, *The State in Capitalist Society* (New York: Basic Books, 1969).

89. Ibid., 182.

90. Ibid., 184.

91. Ibid., 208.

92. Ibid., 214.

93. Ibid., 221.

94. Ibid., 265.

95. Ibid., 266.

96. See, for example, Michael Parenti, *Democracy for the Few* (New York: St. Martin's Press, 1995), chapter 4; and Fred Block, "The Ruling Class Does Not Rule," in *Capitalist Society: Readings for a Critical Sociology*, ed. Richard Quinney (Homewood, IL: Dorsey Press, 1979).

97. James O'Connor, *The Fiscal Crisis of the State* (New York: St. Martin's Press, 1973).

98. See, for example, Mary Francis Berry, *Black Resistance: White Law* (New York: Penguin Books, 1994 [1971]); Ward Churchhill and Jim Vander Wall, *Agents of Repression: The FBI's Secret Wars Against the Black Panther Party and the American Indian Movement* (Boston: South End Press, 1990); James E. Falkowski, *Indian Law/Race Law: A Five Hundred-Year History* (New York: Praeger, 1992); and Alfredo Mirande, *Gringo Justice* (Notre Dame, IN: University of Notre Dame Press, 1987).

99. Harold R. Kerbo, *Social Stratification and Inequality: Class Conflict in Historical and Comparative Perspective*, Second Edition (New York: McGraw-Hill, 1991) 42.

100. Barry Bluestone and Bennett Harrison, *The Deindustrialization of America: Plant Closings, Community Abandonment, and the Dismantling of Basic Industry* (New York: Basic Books, 1982), 158.

101. "Rebuilding to Survive," *Time*, February 16, 1987, 44–45.
102. Donald L. Barlett and James B. Steele, *America: What Went Wrong?* (Kansas City: Andrews and McMeel, 1992), 207.
103. Bluestone and Harrison, *The Deindustrialization of America*, 130.
104. Ibid., 131.
105. Ibid., 133.
106. Ibid., 171–72.
107. Barlett and Steele, *America: What Went Wrong?*, 97, 95.
108. Kevin Phillips, *The Politics of Rich and Poor: Wealth and the American Electorate in the Reagan Aftermath* (New York: Random House, 1990), 94–95.
109. Ibid., 76.
110. Ibid., 78.
111. Ibid., 79.
112. Sylvia Nasar, "The 1980's: A Very Good Time for the Very Rich," *New York Times*, Thursday, March 5, 1992, 1.
113. Barlett and Steele, *America: What Went Wrong?*, 2.
114. Lord Bryce, *American Commonwealth* (1888), cited in Ann Elder and George Kiser, *Governing American States and Communities: Constraints and Opportunities* (Glenview, IL: Scott, Foresman and Co., 1983), 13.
115. Milton C. Cummings, Jr. and David Wise, *Democracy Under Pressure*, Second Edition (New York: Harcourt Brace Jovanovich, 1974), 586.
116. G. William Domhoff, *Who Rules America?* (Englewood Cliffs, NJ: Prentice-Hall, 1967), 132–37.
117. Ruth S. Jones, "Financing State Elections," in *Money and Politics in the United States: Financing Elections in the 1980s*, ed. Michael J. Malbrin (Washington, DC: American Enterprise Institute, 1984), 188.
118. Amitai Etzioni, *Capital Corruption: The New Attack on American Democracy* (New York: Harcourt Brace Jovanovich, 1984), 38.
119. Ibid.
120. Domhoff, *Who Rules America?*, 132–37.
121. Joe R. Feagin and Robert Parker, *Building American Cities: The Urban Real Estate Game* (Englewood Cliffs, NJ: Prentice Hall, 1990), 55–56.
122. Ibid., 56.
123. Ibid.
124. Ibid.

FOUR

STATE LOTTERIES AND THE LEGITIMATION OF INEQUALITY

Economic concentration, deindustrialization, and state policies that favor the interests of the economically powerful have been detrimental for tens of millions of people in the United States. Underemployment, poverty, hunger, and homelessness have increased steadily over the past two decades. The majority teeter precariously, just a paycheck or two from bankruptcy, under enormous household debt. For example, in the early 1950s the average household debt as a percentage of after-tax income was approximately 33 percent. By 1997 it had climbed to almost 95 percent.[1] Not surprisingly, personal bankruptcies in the United States kept pace. Today, tens of thousands of U.S. households are kept afloat financially with the use of high-interest credit cards.[2] Concomitantly, in 1997, 16.1 percent of people in the United States, amounting to 43.4 million people, had no health insurance for the entire year.[3]

Why do people in the United States accept these conditions? Why is it that working and devalued people have demonstrated little discernment of what C. Wright Mills called their "long run, general, and rational interests"?[4] This chapter will go into more detail about the process of legitimation: first, a brief examination of how acceptance of inequality is generally achieved, and then a look at how state lotteries buttress widespread acceptance of the status quo.

The Process of System Legitimation

For the powerful, convincing the masses of people that individual control of great wealth is legitimate is preferable to compelling compliance with an ever-vigilant and costly threat of force. In order for a privileged few to enjoy luxury and extravagance while the many who create the wealth experience hardship, economic marginality, and in-security, individual possession of wealth must be widely accepted as normal and appropriate. This has been true throughout history and remains true today.

The process of legitimation occurs at two levels, a micro- or social psychological level and a macro- or structural level. The relationship between these two levels is dialectical, as they are interdependent and influence one another. At the social psychological level, inequality in the United States has been supported by a general belief in the existence of equal opportunity. According to sociologists, this assumption about the existence of opportunity is at the base of a system-supporting ideology that has been referred to as the dominant stratification ideology, "dominant when it represents the views of those groups which have most of what there is to get."[5] The dominant stratification ideology, reduced to its most basic form, states: (1) there are abundant economic opportunities in the United States; (2) individuals should be industrious and competitive; (3) rewards are, and should be, the result of individual talent and effort; and (4) the distribution of inequality is generally fair and equitable.[6] The pillar of the dominant stratification ideology is belief in opportunity. To the extent that people accept this ideology, individuals are held responsible for their poverty, and sub-stantive threats to the status quo are unlikely.

Research has demonstrated strong public adherence to the domi-nant ideology, which is strongest among the affluent. An analysis of the beliefs of a sample of residents of Muskegon, Michigan, in 1966 found that most respondents believed in the existence of equal opportunity, although those with higher incomes were more likely to believe than lower-income respondents. Higher-income respondents were inclined to hold individuals responsible for their poverty while lower-income people were more likely to question the availability of opportunity.[7]

Similarly, in 1969 a national survey found strong support for individual-level explanations of poverty, with a smaller number of re-spondents, notably lower-income people, young people, and African Americans, giving structural explanations.[8] In 1980 another national study found that, while the majority of respondents continued to adhere to the dominant stratification ideology, the percentage who agreed was declining. The authors of this study cited a 1952 national survey, which found that 88 percent of the respondents agreed with the statement "There's plenty of opportunity and anybody who works hard can go as far as he wants," and noted that the 1966 Muskegon study found that only 78 percent of respondents agreed with the statement. The 1980 survey found that only 70 percent agreed with the statement "There's plenty of opportunity and anybody who works hard can get ahead."[9] Like the earlier studies, the 1980 study also found that lower-income respondents were less likely to accept the dominant ideology than higher-income respondents.[10]

This general belief in the availability of opportunity in the United States supports, and is supported by, the macro- or structural process of legitimation. Recall from the last chapter that Miliband believed that citizens of twentieth-century capitalist societies are indoctrinated to accept values that support existing social arrangements. Miliband's contention is supported by sociological analyses of forces of socialization and control. For example, families, considered by many to be the most powerful agent of socialization, play a powerful role in the legitimation of inequality. Friedrich Engels wrote critically of the family in 1884, viewing it as a social arrangement that oppressed women and children and supported social inequities.[11] Despite the gains produced by the women's movement of the nineteenth and twentieth centuries, families continue to reflect and reinforce gender inequalities.[12] Moreover, many families teach children those values and behaviors considered appropriate and necessary for social adaptability. For example, there is a tendency for working-class parents to teach their children the importance of conformity, while middle-class parents are more likely to emphasize initiative and independence, different orientations that help to reproduce class structures in the next generation.[13]

Religion also plays a role in the legitimation of inequality. Marx viewed religion as the "opium of the people," a powerful narcotic that sedated people and promoted their acquiescence in hardships created by privilege and injustice. Throughout history religion has frequently legitimated social inequality, in many instances by asserting that inequities were the consequence of divine will. Religion has been used, and is still used by some, to justify discrimination and inequality based on gender, race, sexual orientation, and class. While appeals to religious ideals are occasionally used to challenge inequality and legitimate grievances, religion continues to be a significant pillar of the status quo. Charles E. Hurst writes:

> Particularly branches of Christianity ... have legitimated people's beliefs about inequality. Protestantism, in general, which focuses on the individual relationship between each individual and God, stresses the importance of hard work

and equality of opportunity in attaining success.... The "American way" that is so blessed incorporates the values of individualism, freedom, capitalism, and equality of opportunity which make up a core part of the ideology supporting inequality.[14]

The system of education in any society also serves to promote the acceptance of existing arrangements. In most societies students largely are taught to conform to rules and procedures that promote uniformity and control. In the United States they are generally taught to respect hierarchy and to be competitive. History is usually presented in ways that sanitize past injustices and establish a firm basis for the acceptance of existing social arrangements.[15] Reflecting on the educational system, Joe R. Feagin writes:

> Teachers and administrators are important socializers of children. What is taught in school communicates and reinforces basic values and conventional beliefs about United States society. Many teachers, directly or indirectly, teach the ideology of individualism, prevailing conceptions of the poor, positive views of capitalism (less often unions), or stereotypes about minorities and women. Sometimes the formal curriculum communicates beliefs and values supporting the status quo.[16]

The educational system in the United States "looms as one of the more influential purveyors of dominant values."[17]

As Miliband noted, another powerful structural source of legitimation is the mass media. It has been suggested the mass media both support government policy and present views favorable to the interests of the economically powerful.[18] Newspapers throughout the United States are increasingly coming under the control of a relatively small number of corporations,[19] and major television networks are controlled by powerful conglomerates. For example, General Electric purchased the National Broadcasting System (NBC) in 1995. Then, in 1995, the Walt Disney Company conducted one of the largest buyouts in U.S. history by purchasing Capital Cities/ABC Incorporated, which controls the ABC television network and numerous newspapers and radio stations. This transaction created a major convergence of entertainment, news, and multimedia systems. That same year, the media giant Time Warner acquired cable powerhouse Turner Broadcasting. Most recently, in the fall of 1999, Viacom—which owns such cable networks as MTV, VH1, and Nickelodeon, the Paramount film studio, and the Blockbuster video-rental chain—announced its intent to purchase the Columbia Broadcasting System (CBS), a purchase that will create the world's second largest media company, second only to Time Warner. It is predicted that such huge entertainment-communication conglomerates will continue to form and that the thousands of independent cable system operators throughout the country "will be forced out within the next 10 to 12 years, and only five or six companies will remain in business."[20]

This concentrated and centralized control of the major media in the United States exerts a tremendous control over how we see ourselves and the world. For example, it is maintained that news programs in the United States are largely slanted to protect corporate and upper-class interests because (1) much of the news media are owned by the affluent, (2) the mass media are largely dependent on advertising to stay in business and are consequently subject to pressure from corporate sponsors, (3) much news information is provided by government and business experts, and (4) an anticommunism theme is often used to justify corporate and government actions that actually reflect the interests of the privileged.[21] Under these circumstances, for example, corporate mergers, takeovers, and other events that increase economic concentration are generally presented as unrelated and benign occurrences, and their implications for the public or their relationship to systemic trends are seldom analyzed.

Such powerful societal processes—the family, religion, the educational system, the mass media, the state—are among those powerful social institutions that form an organized system of ideas and social arrangements referred to as the *superstructure*. As Marx noted in the nineteenth century, inequality is accepted in large part due to the pervasive system legitimating ideas and processes that confront people as reality. The dominant stratification ideology, promulgated by the superstructure, underlies societal acceptance of dramatic inequality in the United States and sends a disturbing message about, and to, the tens of millions of people living in or near poverty: that they are primarily responsible for their own fate. It is maintained that, through lack of initiative, lack of thrift, lack of talent, or lack of appropriate values, people who do not "make it" have only themselves to blame. This message not only reinforces existing social arrangements but also has devastating psychological consequences for people who blame themselves for their lack of economic success while failing to recognize the deterministic role frequently played by the social structure.[22] They have been taught that capitalism is good, opportunity is plentiful, and all "capable" people should be self-reliant. From this ideological vantage point, the wealthy are glorified and envied and those with few resources are devalued. Attention is diverted from systemic problems and the collective welfare, with the value of individualism elevated above all others. False consciousness is prevalent as most people accept the explanations provided by the dominant ideology for striking inequalities and personal deprivations. As a result, the system is rarely challenged in any meaningful way and the interests of the economically powerful are protected. Although disparities are increasing and belief in opportunity is slipping, state lotteries may be preserving the conservative ideology, especially among many who otherwise are least likely to believe it.

Lotteries as the New Opportunity

At a time when chances for economic security are declining for most people in society, the state lottery stands out as a *new opportunity* for individual economic advancement. The mass media has been widely used to legitimate and promote lottery play, and states send the message that a life-altering opportunity is only one dollar away. State lotteries are now largely viewed as a normal, rational, and acceptable way for people to pursue their hopes and dreams. Widely publicized stories of lottery winners, like the bankrupt, fifty-two-year-old telephone installer, David Demarest, whose "life had changed in more happy ways than even he anticipated"; or the police officer and waitress whose shared lottery jackpot brought them love and happiness in the film *It Could Happen To You*; or the fictional lottery winner Claire Goddard, a woman previously of "modest means," who went on a spending spree buying luxury cars and mansions—all send dramatic messages to the public that opportunity still exists, for everyone.

A study conducted by the author provides some empirical support for the contention that state lotteries—specifically the Superlotto—are related to perceptions of economic opportunity in the United States. A 1992 survey of 450 randomly selected adult residents of a small midwestern city found that 77 percent had played the state lottery. For 63 percent of this group, the Superlotto was the game of choice. Interestingly, more than 45 percent of respondents believed the most likely way they would achieve wealth would be to win it—and 94 percent of this group believed they would most likely win it through the lottery. Those most likely to put their chances with the lottery were older than forty, did not have high-school diplomas, and had incomes less than $40,000 a year. Importantly, it was found that 77 percent of the respondents who played the Superlotto game believed that America is the "land of opportunity," compared to only 61 percent of those who reported a preference for instant games and other lottery games with more modest prizes.[23] These results provide evidence that state lotteries are now a consequential aspect of people's beliefs about opportunity and their hopes for economic advancement. This contention is further supported by the words of a lottery player in a letter to the editor of a magazine called *Lotto World*: "Lotteries ... create a level playing field for each of us who dares to buy a ticket."[24]

Lotteries and the Acquisition of Wealth

A primary theme in state lottery advertisements is that acquisition of wealth is a wonderful, transcendent experience—and that the opportunity is available to all. For example, an Illinois lottery television commercial showed images of a huge mansion with the following voice-over:

> In America we do not have kings nor queens or even dukes. What we have is far more democratic. It is called Superlotto and it gives each individual a chance for untold wealth. So play Superlotto because, even though you can't be born a king, no one said you can't live like one.

Similarly, Charles T. Clotfelter and Philip J. Cook observed:

> A California television commercial for an instant game called *The Good Life* touts the advantages of wealth with images of an elegantly dressed couple dancing, a woman walking expensive dogs, a red carpet being unrolled, and a couple on a yacht. A Michigan ad puts it simply: "The rich. Join them."[25]

In December 1998, the U.K. National Lottery ceremoniously boasted that in the four years since its creation it had enabled 710 people to "join the rich" by making them millionaires.[26]

In their frenzy to sell lottery tickets, governments are promoting the desirability of wealth just as much as the television program *Lifestyles of the Rich and Famous* and every other program, film, book, and magazine that glamorizes and legitimates indulgence. By dangling before the public expensive cars, yachts, and even, in the case of the New York lottery, a mansion so extravagant that a fictional one had to be created, state governments are directly promoting what the turn-of-the-century sociologist Thorstein Veblen called "conspicuous consumption."[27] Veblen viewed the long-held infatuation with wealth in capitalist

society as a carry-over from earlier periods in human history he characterized as "barbarian." In such societies people relegated to the
positions of peasants and slaves performed work that was indispensable
to the survival of the community, but they were exploited by priests,
chieftains, and other members of the "leisure class." Veblen noted that
excess consumption of quality goods and ostentatious displays of wealth
go well beyond satisfying individual physical needs and instead become
symbols of one's rank and status and "superior character." Conversely,
the "low-grade character" of those who live at subsistence levels are
made similarly obvious to all. As Veblen noted,

> Since the consumption of these more excellent goods is an evidence of wealth,
> it becomes honorific; and conversely, the failure to consume in due quantity and
> quality becomes a mark of inferiority and demerit.[28]

Veblen viewed conspicuous consumption as "waste" because such a
pattern of consumption "does not serve human life or human well-
being on the whole."[29] Veblen suggested that these anachronistic values
and standards of human worth were particularly problematic in the
later nineteenth century because they served to detract many from the
industry and hard effort necessary to sustain industrial society.

Veblen's ideas warrant consideration, especially today. In the late
twentieth century, a time when the human population is growing at a
prodigious rate, natural resources are being rapidly depleted, increasing
numbers of people in the United States and throughout the world are
living at subsistence levels, and millions of laboring people continue to
have the value of their labor expropriated, is it rational public policy
for state governments to extol the virtues of private accumulation of
great wealth? Whose responsibility is it to consider these questions and
to integrate them into the realm of public discourse? Certainly, questions concerning the general welfare and public interest are not given
much consideration by governments, lottery officials, or advertising
executives, whose basic focus and goal is the continuous increase in
lottery ticket sales. When such questions are considered, they are asked
at the federal level—and usually produce few results, as evidenced by
recent events in the U.K. and the U.S., as we will see in Chapter 5.

Lotteries as Diversion

Reflecting on the social consequences of state lotteries, H. Roy Kaplan
remarked:

> This illusory dream [of great wealth from the lottery] can also be used as a method of social control—to placate people by diverting attention from their misfortunes and meaningless lives. This social control aspect of lotteries and legalized gambling assumes greater significance as they proliferate.[30]

State lotteries help to divert attention people's attention from their troubles and misgivings, while serving as a safety valve, siphoning stress and frustration into a system-enhancing activity and thus helping to avert the potential threat of a mass uprising. Furthermore, lotteries also help to divert attention from problems and social arrangements that affect people's lives. Questions about who makes major economic decisions, why certain decisions are made, why the quality of life is slipping, why working conditions are frequently tedious and unrewarding, and related questions, are seldom publicly contemplated in meaningful ways.

This diversion of focus is troubling when one considers that education and the fairness of societal arrangements are necessary for the development of social and economic justice. Marx believed that people oppressed by the social order would eventually recognize their collective interests and act to change the system. Bertell Ollman suggested that traditional Marxian theory generally views wage earners as a

> class of people whose conditions of life, whose experiences at work and else- where, whose common struggles and discussions will sooner or later bring them to a consciousness of their state and of what must be done to transform it.[31]

There is evidence that people with low incomes today are inclined to challenge aspects of the economic order. This traditional Marxist tenet is supported if we recall that people with lower incomes are somewhat less likely than higher-income people totally to accept conventional explanations of inequality. We saw, for example, that people with lower incomes are less accepting of the dominant stratification ideology and more inclined to believe individual problems are caused by the social structure. Moreover, the 1992 study of the small midwestern city cited earlier also compared the responses of people in different income categories on several questions regarding economic policies. People with low and moderate incomes were more likely than higher income respondents to favor (1) placing limits on income, (2) government ownership of basic industries, (3) government guarantee of jobs for everyone, (4) the democratization of corporate decision-making, and (5) socialist participation in economic decision-making— all at levels of statistical significance.[32]

State lotteries, however, are among those forces that mitigate against this inclination to challenge the economic structure. We saw that 77 percent of the respondents in the 1992 study had played the lottery, and people who prefer the Superlotto—constituting the majority of state lottery players—express strong agreement with the statement "America is the land of opportunity where anyone who works hard can get ahead." Moreover, those respondents who pinned their hopes of wealth on winning the lottery were disproportionately people with low levels of education and income. Consequently, state lotteries have joined those other powerful superstructural forces that stifle the formation of a political consciousness among people with low and moderate incomes.

People with lower incomes are not the only group whose potential inclination to push for social change is muted by state lotteries. The young frequently play an important role in the promotion of social change.[33] Young people are better able to be proponents of change if they can assess critically the conditions and ideologies that confront them. Bertell Ollman notes:

> [I]t is possible to fight against the character structure of workers by fighting against its construction, by counteracting the disorienting influence of family, school, and church, whatever in fact makes it difficult for the individual once [he/she] becomes an adult to make an objective assessment of [her/his] oppression and to act against it.
> The concrete aims of this radical activity ... are to get teenage and even younger members of the working class to question the existing order along with all its leaders and symbols, to loosen generalized habits of respect and obedience, to oppose whatever doesn't make sense in terms of their needs as individuals and as members of a group.[34]

There is little indication that the youth of the United States in the late twentieth century possess the historical, sociopolitical, or economic knowledge to counteract the contemporary ideology and its "disorienting influence." Socialized by educational and media systems that champion the status quo, millions of young people have come of age in a society where debates about the merits of great wealth are almost nonexistent and where state government inducements to gamble precede their birth. Not surprisingly, states have been known to target lottery games and advertisements at young people. For example, the aim of Oregon's Sports Action games was to increase participation among young men, and the Ohio lottery created television ads showing young people admiring expensive cars and yachts to the Hall and Oates pop song "You Make My Dreams Come True."

Thus the superstructure of U.S. society does little to arouse organized dissent among the nation's youth, and the lottery further undermines the development of political consciousness in young people by glorifying wealth and material acquisition through the promotion of lottery tickets. Moreover, as we saw in the preceding chapter, some experts are very concerned with the increase in gambling among young people, and one professional believes gambling problems have surpassed drug-related problems among teenagers.

Lotteries and the Denigration of Work

Another message promoted by state lotteries that is particularly effective at selling tickets is the undesirability of work. For example, several Ohio lottery winners were featured in advertisements that reflected anti-work values. One winner comments.

> Everybody talks about, "I'm not going to work tomorrow—if I don't show up, I won the Lotto." I *won* the Lotto and I *didn't* go to work today.

Another winner says.

> Eight years ago—the first thought that went through my mind was that I didn't have to go to work today—and I didn't for seven years.

Alan J. Karcher discusses an advertisement for the New Jersey lottery that

> showed a popcorn and soda vendor working at a ball game trying to deal with three customers at once. With a terribly harried look on his face, his hat askew, and his tray about to fall, the message reads, "If I win Pick 6, I won't have to do this any more." These print ads were just part of a general advertising campaign, whose principle message was this: Jobs requiring physical labor won't be necessary if you win the lottery. A series of half-completed billboards went up with a message scrawled reading: "I don't have to do this job! I just won the lottery."[35]

Lottery promoters are shrewd in their validation of worker dissatisfaction. Marx believed that meaningful work is important for human beings because it can be a creative and satisfying experience necessary for individual development and happiness. However, he maintained that under capitalism the process of work became alienating and hostile. Increasing automation and loss of worker control resulted in people becoming distanced from the finished product of their labor and isolated from other workers, with whom they were made to be competitors. Work became an alienating experience in which workers also became estranged from their own creative nature and potential.

The degradation of work has increased under capitalism in the twentieth century.[36] Many people occupy jobs that allow for little autonomy, participation in decision-making, or other characteristics that make work meaningful and rewarding. Consequently, many find work to be a tedious, dehumanizing, and sometimes dangerous experience.[37] A recent national study of employee attitudes found that millions of workers throughout the United States feel ignored by company managers. Almost two-thirds yearned to become more involved in decisions that affected their companies or places of employment; most do not protest because they fear they are expendable.[38]

The trying working conditions experienced by millions of people in the United States are compounded further by the loss of decent-paying jobs as the result of deindustrialization, mega-mergers, and the continuing process of automation. This loss of jobs has been accompanied by a significant increase in lower-paying, service-sector jobs and part-time jobs, thus expanding the numbers of the working poor.[39] Many of the "lucky" ones who have managed to survive corporate mergers and downsizing and retain their positions now quietly struggle with heavier work loads, fearful of falling victim to new rounds of employee cutbacks. Under these conditions, loaded with stress, anxiety, and hardship, it is not surprising that many people feel estranged from their work.

A logical and rational strategy for workers would be to organize themselves and promote democratic workplaces that allow for the promotion of decent wages, job security, worker participation in decision-making, and the creation of more meaningful and safer working environments. However, the possibility for such organization and action is reduced by lottery advertisements that validate worker unhappiness but which provide an individualistic and system-defending answer—*play the lottery, become rich and quit your job.*

Moreover, state lotteries deprecate people with low incomes in advertisements that portray lower-income status as inferior, to be remedied *only* by the acquisition of wealth. Lottery advertisements frequently juxtapose images of great wealth with scenes that depict people who are not wealthy as second-rate. Clotfelter and Cook noted:

> The District of Columbia ran a series of before-and-after ads.... In one such print ad the "before" picture shows a bedraggled man, face covered with stubble,

hair matted down, wearing glasses and sloppy clothes. In the "after" picture he is clean shaven, well groomed, wearing a tuxedo but no glasses, conspicuously holding a copy of a theater program. The ad proclaims, "Just One Ticket … and It Could Happen To You."[40]

Such messages from state lotteries do a great disservice to the millions of people with modest incomes whose hard work and labor continue to generate the goods and services essential for the survival of the society. However, they are not surprising. People with limited social, economic, or political power have long been devalued in the United States, and used as scapegoats for social problems since the advancement of social Darwinism.[41] Lottery ads reinforce this perception through their defamation of people with few resources and their promulgation of the view that individuals with wealth merit public adulation and envy.

State lotteries are now major practitioners of the custom of celebrating the privileged and devaluing people with few resources—what will be referred to here as the "Ratchet–Cratchit Syndrome" in honor of Ebenezer Scrooge's much-abused clerk in Charles Dickens's *A Christmas Carol*. This syndrome simultaneously exalts the privileged and subjects laboring people to grinding social and psychological denigration. It also severely restricts political mobilization because it contributes to the constant divisions and conflicts among those devalued members of society who compete with each other for jobs, housing, and other necessities. Today, as in the past, social groups whose economic interests are closely related continue to compete for crumbs and desperately try to advance their social status in relation to other, "really inferior" people—often those who are different because of their ethnic background, sexual orientation, or gender. In their efforts to distance themselves socially from other unjustly defamed groups, oppressed people unwittingly continue to reinforce those values and social arrangements that underlie their oppression. As Holly Sklar observes:

> The cycle of unequal opportunity is intensifying. Its beneficiaries often slander those most systematically undervalued, underpaid, underemployed, underfinanced, underinsured, underrated and otherwise underserved and undermined—as undeserving and underclass, impoverished in moral values and lacking the proper "work ethic."
>
> The angry, shrinking middle class is misled into thinking that those lower on the economic ladder are pulling them down, when in reality those on top are rising at the expense of those below. People who should be working together to transform the economic policies that are hurting them are instead turning hatefully on each other.[42]

The Ratchet–Cratchit messages promulgated by state lotteries feed these misconceptions. Unfortunately, unlike in Dickens's tale, where Scrooge's Christmas Eve visions suddenly make him kindly and generous to Cratchit, and everyone else he sees, the lives of people in the United States will not improve so quickly. Rather, as history has demonstrated repeatedly, improvements in the quality of life for people are typically the result of years of struggle.[43] Moreover, the collective political consciousness necessary to catalyze an early twenty-first-century struggle for social justice is further hampered by yet another alienating aspect of state lotteries—superstition and magic.

State Lotteries Promote Superstition

Lottery games such as Superlotto provide a measure of buyer participation by allowing ticket buyers to select numbers instead of participating in a passive random drawing. Statistically, since every possible outcome has the same probability of winning, players cannot actually increase the probability of winning by selecting their own numbers. However, players may not know or believe this. Indeed, as one lottery critic in the U.K. observed, "[g]overnment initiative … has done the most to undermine the public understanding of statistics: The National Lottery."[44] Allowing players to select their own numbers creates a perception of increased control that helps increase participation. Ticket buyers use various methods to select numbers, often relying on some form of superstition. Many ticket buyers seek to select "lucky" numbers, frequently based on birthdays or anniversary dates or derived from dreams.

An entire industry has emerged to help would-be lottery winners find their "lucky numbers." Players can buy an array of pamphlets and books or consult one of countless "psychics and mystics" who are available to help them get lucky—for a fee. For example, the following advertisement appeared in the magazine *LottoWorld*:

Your Direct Connection
To Your Lucky Numbers!

Lottoworld's Psychic Connection

Our Dynamic Line-up
of Psychics, Astrologers and Numerologists
give you their daily picks for Pick 3, 4, 5, 6 and Powerball

A new set of weekly predictions updated
every day by our lottery experts
$1.49 per minute[45]

The cover of another issue of *LottoWorld* featured "The Amazing Kreskin" holding a lottery form to his forehead.

In Ohio, a leaflet selling for $1.75 called *Ohio Daily Number Handbook: Lucky Numbers* gives readers suggestions on how to determine their "lucky numbers," and it lists lucky numbers selected by the "Mysterious Strategy Man." The text reads:

> This man is noted for his unerring accuracy in deciphering the numerical mysteries of the atmosphere, both within and beyond ourselves. Inspired by the incense of his lamp, his mind drifts and explores the dreams of all who pass his way, translating each thought into it's numerical significance. This amazing power to interpret dreams into numerology has astonished people for 3,000 years. The Mysterious Strategy Man is the latest in a long line of Mystics who have benefited mankind.[46]

The following story appeared in the July 1995 edition of the *Bull's Eye Lottery Book*, a thirty-page booklet selling for $1.75 that lists "lucky numbers" for specific names and zodiac signs:

> *New Orleans*—Down-and-out mom Mimi Dealah was dead broke and desperate till she won a whopping $2 million lottery jackpot—two days after praying at the grave of famed voodoo priestess Marie Laveau....
>
> "I was desperate. My husband died last year and left nothing but a pile of unpaid bills and it was a struggle just to feed my three kids.
>
> "Then my friend here in New Orleans suggested I come visit her and make a trip to Marie Laveau's grave." And two days after that fateful trip, the elated lady learned that she'd won just over $2 million in a multi-state lottery.
>
> "I don't know how she did it, but I think they should make Marie Laveau a saint," said mystified Mimi.[47]

This tendency for people to resort to superstition in their efforts to achieve economic security is not just a by-product of state government policy. As Clotfelter and Cook observed,

> Instead of providing information that would be helpful in parimutuel games, the lottery agencies appear to be interested in encouraging rather than dispelling the fallacy that numbers are important for their own sake. While most have introduced a random selection option for on-line games, they continue to foster player loyalty to personal lucky numbers.[48]

Many states continuously exhort people to "play your lucky number." This advice fosters alienation by reinforcing the notion that some supernatural force can determine their economic fate.

Perhaps the modern-day reliance on superstition is to be expected. In some respects, the ordeal experienced by people today in one of the wealthiest and most scientifically advanced nations in the world trying to feed, clothe, house, and otherwise sustain themselves is similar to that faced by their early ancestors who also relied on superstition and magic.

In earlier societies where people relied heavily on climatic conditions for life-sustaining harvests, people used various forms of magical manipulation to try to affect the weather and environment, elements over which they really had no control. In the face of their helplessness, they used various types of incantations and rituals to appeal to supernatural and spiritual forces, creating the illusion that they could exert at least a modicum of control over their fate. With the advent of science and technology, humankind has developed the potential to exert a considerable degree of control over the forces that affect our lives. Indeed, in the face of expanding scientific knowledge, many regard magic and superstition as irrational, delusional, and anachronistic.

Still, in the late twentieth century, magic and superstition abound. This reliance on the supernatural is not surprising, however, when millions of people experience such a precarious economic existence. They are estranged from an economic system that can take away their jobs, homes, and health care—if they have secured such necessities— with the apparent arbitrariness of a random act of nature. Certainly, most have no more control over a corporate decision to merge, downsize, or relocate operations than they do over the weather. For some, like those who preceded them centuries earlier, this feeling of dependence and uncertainty is eased and a modicum of perceived control is achieved by resorting to magic and superstition. Encouraged by state governments, millions today concentrate on finding those elusive "lucky numbers" that can bestow security and respect. The need for, and state encouragement of, superstition in the late twentieth century raises serious issues about both the rationality and the ethics of economic and political policy in the United States.

Postscript

While the author was doing research for this book, he went into a convenience store to buy copies of *LottoWorld*, the *Ohio Daily Number Handbook*, and the *Bull's Eye Lottery Book*. The woman working behind the counter asked if he was trying to win the lottery; he replied that he was doing some research and believed the advice and information contained in the booklets were bogus. The woman said that she followed the advice offered in these publications, frequently playing the lucky numbers associated with her zodiac sign. He suggested to her that this strategy would probably not increase her chances of winning, to which she angrily replied, "I've got just as much chance of winning as anybody else." In retrospect, this exchange challenged the woman's sense of control, and she responded in a predictably defensive way. Her response, however, validates a theory about system legitimation and social control in the twentieth century offered by Herbert Marcuse. While systems of injustice in the past occasionally saw people reject unconvincing ideologies and attempt revolts and rebellions in challenge to the power and excesses of the privileged, armed soldiers stood ready to turn them back. However, in late-twentieth-century capitalist society, system-challenging actions are largely nonexistent. Writing in 1969, Marcuse pondered the following question:

> At this stage, the question is no longer: how can the individual satisfy his needs without hurting others, but rather: how can he satisfy his own needs without hurting himself, without reproducing, through his aspirations and satisfactions, his dependence on an exploitative apparatus which, in satisfying his needs, perpetuates his servitude?[49]

Marcuse's reflection in 1969 becomes even more relevant today with the proliferation of state lotteries in the United States. Like the woman working at the convenience store who apparently had invested part of her hopes and dreams in the lottery, millions like her have found a new attachment to the status quo, the chance of becoming a millionaire. While a tiny number will succeed, the vast majority do not need armed soldiers to keep them from seeking their "long run, general, and rational interests." Their conservative socialization, coupled with state-sponsored lottomania, secure their fidelity to a system that offers wealth for a few, and hardships and insecurity for the many.

Notes

1. "Squeezing Debtors," *Left Business Observer*, 84 (July 21, 1998), 1–2.
2. Ibid., 1–2.
3. Laura Meckler (Associated Press), *Survey: Many Americans Still Lack Health Insurance*. http://cnn.com/ALLPOLITICS/stories/1998/10/19/hmo.ap/ (1998).
4. C. Wright Mills, *The Marxists* (New York, 1962) 115; reprinted in *Capitalist Society: Readings for a Critical Sociology*, ed. Richard Quinney (Homewood, IL: Dorsey Press, 1979), 170.
5. Joan Huber and William H. Form, *Income and Ideology: An Analysis of the American Political Formula* (New York: Free Press, 1973), 2.

6. Robert A. Rothman, *Inequality and Stratification: Class, Color, and Gender*, Second Edition (Englewood Cliffs, NJ: Prentice Hall, 1993), 57.

7. Huber and Form, *Income and Ideology*.

8. Joe R. Feagin, "When It Comes to Poverty, It Is Still 'God Helps Those Who Help Themselves'," *Psychology Today*, 6 (1972), 101–29.

9. See James R. Kluegel and Eliot R. Smith, *Beliefs About Inequality: Americans' Views of What Is and What Ought to Be* (Hawthorne, NY: Aldine De Gruyter, 1986), 43–45.

10. Ibid.

11. Friedrich Engels, *The Origin of the Family, Private Property and the State* (New York: Penguin Books, 1972 [1884]).

12. See Randall Collins, *Sociology of Marriage and the Family: Gender, Love and Property* (Chicago: Nelson Hall, 1985); and Carol Smart, *The Ties That Bind: Law, Marriage and the Reproduction of Patriarchal Relations* (London: Routledge & Kegan Paul, 1984).

13. Melvin L. Kohn, *Class and Conformity*, Second Edition (Homewood, IL: Dorsey Press, 1977).

14. Charles E. Hurst, *Social Inequality: Forms, Causes, and Consequences* (Boston: Allyn & Bacon, 1992), 303–04.

15. See, for example, Samuel Bowles and Herbert Gintis, *Schooling in Capitalist America: Education Reforms and the Contradictions of Economic Life* (New York: Basic Books, 1976).

16. Joe R. Feagin, *Social Problems: A Critical Power-Conflict Perspective*, Second Edition (Englewood Cliffs, NJ: Prentice Hall, 1986), 199.

17. Michael Parenti, *Democracy for the Few*, Fifth Edition (New York: St. Martin's Press, 1988), 37.

18. G. William Domhoff, *The Powers That Be* (New York: Vintage, 1979); and Thomas R. Dye, *Who's Running America? The Reagan Years* (Englewood Cliffs, NJ: Prentice Hall, 1983).

19. See Michael Parenti, *Inventing Reality: The Politics of the Mass Media* (New York: St. Martin's Press, 1986); and Ben H. Bagdikian, *The Media Monopoly* (Boston: Beacon Press, 1987).

20. This prediction comes from Jim Sayer, Professor of Communications at Wright State University. He was cited in the *Dayton Daily News* on August 1, 1995, 1.

21. Edward S. Herman and Noam Chomsky, *Manufacturing Consent: The Political Economy of the Mass Media* (New York: Pantheon, 1988).

22. See William Ryan, *Blaming the Victim* (New York: Vintage, 1976); and Michael Lewis, *The Culture of Inequality* (Amherst: University of Massachusetts Press, 1978).

23. David Nibert, "State Lotteries and Perceptions of Opportunities" (Paper presented at the Annual Meeting of the American Sociological Association, Los Angeles, August 1994).

24. *LottoWorld*, July 24, 1995, 10.

25. Charles T. Clotfelter and Philip Cook, *Selling Hope: State Lotteries in America* (Cambridge, MA: Harvard University Press, 1989), 207–08.

26. *Electronic Telegraph*, "Lottery Adds 226 to List of Millionaires," December 28, 1998, 1, http://www.telegraph.co.uk.

27. Thorstein Veblen, *The Theory of the Leisure Class* (New York: Penguin Books,

1979 [1899]).
28. Ibid., 74, 84.
29. Ibid., 97.
30. H. Roy Kaplan, "The Social and Economic Impact of State Lotteries," *Annals of the American Academy of Political and Social Science,* 474 (July 1984), 104.
31. Bertell Ollman, "Toward Class Consciousness in the Working Class," *Politics and Society,* 3 (Fall 1972); reprinted in *Capitalist Society,* ed. Quinney, 170.
32. David Nibert, "An Examination of the Dominant Stratification Ideology in the Post-Reagan Era" (Paper presented at the Annual Meeting of the American Sociological Association, Washington DC, August 1995).
33. See Robert H. Lauer, *Perspectives on Social Change* (Boston: Allyn and Bacon, 1982), 262–73.
34. Ollman, "Toward Class Consciousness in the Working Class," 184.
35. Alan J. Karcher, *Lotteries* (New Brunswick, NJ: Transaction, 1992), 76–77.
36. See Harry Braverman, *Labor and Monopoly Capital: The Degradation of Work in the Twentieth Century* (New York: Monthly Review Press, 1975); and Craig Calhoun, "The Political Economy of Work," in *Political Economy: A Critique of American Society,* ed. Scott G. McNall (Glenview, IL: Scott, Foresman & Co.,1981), 272–99.
37. See, for example, Jeffrey Reiman, *The Rich Get Richer and the Poor Get Prison: Ideology, Crime and Criminal Justice* (Needham Heights, MA: Allyn and Bacon, 1995), 70–76.
38. Susan Dentzer, "Anti-Union, But Not Anti-Unity," *U.S. News and World Report,* July 1995, 17.
39. Robert J. Sheak, "U.S. Capitalism, 1972–1992: The Jobs Problem," *Critical Sociology,* 21, no. 1 (1995), 33–57.
40. Clotfelter and Cook, *Selling Hope,* 207.
41. See, for example, David Nibert, "The Political Economy of Developmental Disability," *Critical Sociology,* 21, no. 1 (1995), 59–80.
42. Holly Sklar, *Chaos or Community? Seeking Solutions, Not Scapegoats, for Bad Economics* (Boston: South End Press, 1995), 2–3.
43. See, for example, Frances Fox Piven and Richard Cloward, *Poor People's Movements: Why They Succeed, How They Fail* (New York: Pantheon, 1977).
44. Roger Highfield, "Editors of the Paranormal in a Flutter Over Angels and the Lottery," *Electronic Telegraph,* January 22, 1997, 2, http://www.telegraph.co.uk.
45. *LottoWorld,* July 10, 1995, 70.
46. *Ohio Daily Number Handbook: Lucky Numbers,* 179 (July 1995).
47. *Bull's Eye Lottery Book,* July 1995, 22–23.
48. Clotfelter and Cook, *Selling Hope,* 89.
49. Herbert Marcuse, *An Essay on Liberation* (Boston: Beacon Press, 1969), 4.

FIVE

A LOTTO OBSTACLES
TO CHANGE

For myself, I have never believed that "all history" can or must be explained in economic terms ... Yet, it has seemed to me, and does now, that in the great transformations of society ... economic "forces" [are] primordial or fundamental, and come nearer to "explaining" events than any other "forces."

Charles A. Beard[1]

It has been nearly forty years since Louis Hamod was arrested for possession of state lottery tickets. During that time the legal status and public image of lotteries have been remade, and lotteries now are a common part of the socioeconomic landscape. The voices of lottery critics have been muted in a culture where state game promotions and results are now daily features in newspapers and television news programs.

Such pervasive cultural acceptance and approval of state lotteries are bolstered by the belief that they are a harmless and entertaining diversion that adds funds to public education. And many, especially those with lower incomes and lower levels of education, believe state lotteries are the most likely vehicle for them to realize their dreams. Most people would view lotteries in a much different way, however, if our society cultivated an informed citizenry and revealed the historical, political, and economic underpinning of the manufactured reality in which they are so deeply immersed. But, as Marx and numerous later scholars have pointed out, such is not the way of societies characterized by profound disparities in the distribution of wealth and income. Thus, without the opportunity or ability to see the relationship between social structural arrangements and "individual" problems, most people remain prisoners of their times and culture, in terms not only of experiences and opportunities but also of consciousness. In 1978 the late

Carl Sagan wrote: "Our children ... have been taught the answers before most of them ... have had an opportunity even to formulate the questions."[2]

By way of summation, one of the basic points developed in the preceding chapters is that material/economic circumstances exert a profound effect on what occurs in a society. Thus, we saw the social disruption that accompanied the shift from manorial to capitalist economic arrangements facilitated the first use of lotteries as a capital-raising device. Those most drawn to the early lotteries were primarily those who labored. Their dreams of security and happiness were taxed in order to fund the expansions and extravagances of early capitalism. In the nineteenth-century United States, despite ethical condemnation, lotteries were not abolished until they were no longer needed to raise capital.

Although lotteries were outlawed, economic exploitation and injustice continued into the twentieth century, and many voices challenged capitalism itself. Pressure from labor unions, rights movements, and a myriad of reformers and revolutionaries altered the distribution of resources somewhat earlier in the twentieth century; some of the worst abuses were relieved, and utter desperation for many was staved off by minimal entitlement programs. However, many reforms were later dismantled or reduced in scope or funding with the advent of the new era of global economic competition that arose later in the century—prompting a return to social policies that accentuate individualism and self-help.

This reassertion of the "rugged individualism" of the past is particularly hard in a nation that has been transformed from one where people once were mainly self-employed to one where most are on a payroll, with little prospect for control of their economic destinies. At the same time, the opportunities for gainful employment have decreased for millions of workers with the coming of a new economic order and its tendencies toward automation, deindustrialization, capital flight, buy-outs, mergers, and downsizing. Those who were poor or economically marginal, as well as the millions who believed they were part of the comfortable middle class, became victims of economic and structural circumstances, much like many of their predecessors who were caught in the wheels of early capitalism. Also like those who went before them, many seek salvation through lottery play.

It has always been in the interest of those who control wealth to attribute responsibility for the resulting social ills to others—usually those who are socially devalued and less able to defend themselves. This victim-blaming tactic flourishes in the contemporary United States and helps to prevent the reemergence of the social justice and collectivist movements that were seen earlier in the century. Moreover, racism, sexism, classism, and other pervasive ideologies are fueled by continued economic uncertainty and fear. Although perhaps not deliberately plotted by the elite, such prejudices unquestionably assist the maintenance of the status quo by providing scapegoats for economic ills and creating factions and rivals from a large percentage of the citizenry who might otherwise unite to challenge the prevailing order.

Meanwhile, the importance and virtues of the wealthy are paraded before the masses, while the poor are vilified on a daily basis. As a result, millions who experience poverty and deprivation view their circumstances as personal and even deserved. The perceived "naturalness" of this state of affairs, and supportive ideals of individual responsibility, are cultivated and supported by messages delivered through family life, schools, churches, the mass media, peers, and the state.

Lotteries thus fit very nicely into the established societal superstructure. Once viewed by many as a public scourge, they have been reintroduced, marketed, and made acceptable by being wrapped in cultural icons and ideals. Lotteries are trumpeted as a form of opportunity, especially for those who are economically marginalized and trapped by financial uncertainty. Lottery marketing denigrates work, glorifies great wealth, and distracts people from the true source of many of their problems—the high degree of concentration of wealth. Lottery promoters exhort the masses to try their luck at that chance of joining the ranks of the privileged. In essence, low- and moderate-income people are invited to become players in the "mother of all" crap games—capitalism. While they may have little to gamble in stock markets or on commodity futures, they risk ever-increasing percentages of their modest incomes on what a 1934 *Christian Century* article called "the most cruel kind of financial malpractice."[3] Most, however, do not realize that the large-scale participants in the financial markets and other capitalist institutions in fact are not gambling as much as it may seem; the game has been rigged so that their risks are minimal and their safety frequently is guaranteed by public bailouts. Meanwhile, the lottery promoters' encouragement of public belief in superstition and magic compounds social alienation and further insulates the powerful from the potential threat of an educated, informed, and activist majority.

We have also seen that the state functions to preserve and enhance capitalism and complements those forces that legitimate the disparities endemic to the system. This role of the state is masked and not obvious to many because the state plays a complicated role in contemporary society. Nearly everyone benefits in some ways from some state activities. Nonetheless, the state's useful and beneficial undertakings occur within a program that legitimates, protects, and expands the interests of the wealthy.

As we have seen, federal policies created budget crises for state governments and also increased demand among the public for lotteries by actions that facilitated profit accumulation in the new global order. Tax code changes, deregulation, and generous government subsidies facilitated corporate mergers and corporate flight and enhanced corporate bargaining power relative to that of state governments and workers. In the face of circumstances that are corporate-friendly, but disastrous to citizens and communities, state governments—with no little assistance from profit-minded, lottery-related businesses—turned to lotteries as a tool of public finance. Of course, the decision by state governments to reestablish lotteries was motivated by economic circumstances and not from a conscious desire or conspiracy to hurt people who are economically marginal or poor. As Charles Horton Cooley once observed,

In the same way the wrongs that afflict society are seldom willed by any one or any group, but are by-products of acts of will having other objects; they are done, as someone has said, rather with the elbows than the fists.[4]

So, in the last analysis, state lotteries, a regressive form of taxation contributing to compulsive gambling and belief in magic, while represented falsely as serving the interests of children, were created by state governments due to economic ills brought on by self-serving policies of the wealthy.

It could be argued that this critical, unflattering perspective on state lotteries unfairly reproaches the United States, when many other Western democracies also have government-sponsored lotteries. In truth, all other Western industrial nations are capitalistic and consequently experience disparities in the distribution of resources. However, citizens in the United States appear to suffer more than those in other Western countries from the dynamics of late-twentieth-century capitalism. For example, a 1991 study conducted by the Joint Center for Political and Economic Studies found that the "United States has more poverty and is less able to cope with it than any other major industrialized Western democracy."[5] Compared to Canada, Great Britain, West Germany, the Netherlands, France, Italy, and Sweden, the study found that poverty in the United States is more widespread and severe and that U.S. government programs are the least able to lift families with children out of poverty. The study found that the United States is the only Western democracy that "has failed to give a significant proportion of its poor population a measure of income security."[6] A 1995 study comparing disparities in wealth among industrialized nations found that

> the growing concentration of American wealth and income challenge a cherished part of the country's self-image: They show that, rather than being an egalitarian society, the United States has become the most economically stratified of industrial nations.
>   Even class societies like Britain, which inherited large differences in income and wealth over centuries going back to their feudal pasts, now have greater economic equality than the United States.[7]

The 1995 study found that the richest 1 percent of households in the United States control about 40 percent of the nation's wealth— twice as much as in Great Britain, the country with the greatest inequality in Western Europe. In Germany, high-wage families earn about 2.5 times as much as low-wage families, and that differential has been shrinking. In comparison, in the United States high-wage families earn more than four times as much as low-wage, and the difference is increasing.[8] This study prompted an editorial response from the *New York Times* pointing out that "excessive inequality can break the spirit of those trapped in society's cellar—and exacerbate social tensions."[9]

The comparatively high levels of poverty and of economic disparity in the United States are further compounded by the fact that the country lags far behind other nations in welfare spending. The U.S. ranks well below the Netherlands, France, Sweden, Italy, and eleven other industrialized nations in its overall spending on welfare as a percentage of national income.[10] Compared to sixty-three other industrialized nations, the United States is the only one without some form of guaranteed income program for all families in need; it also is the only Western democracy without some form of comprehensive national health care for all citizens.[11] Accordingly, although government-sponsored lotteries everywhere are subject to criticism for the problems they spawn and their basic unfairness, the proliferation of state lotteries in the United States is most problematic because the "consumer demand" for them is fueled by a higher level of deprivation and insecurity than exists in most other industrialized countries.

Further reason to scrutinize closely lotteries in the United States comes from an examination of lottery sales worldwide. In 1998, the United States accounted for 34 percent of all worldwide lottery sales.[12] The disproportionate level of lottery ticket sales in the United States can be attributed both to the high level of lottomania promoted by state governments and to the large number of people seeking to escape economic uncertainty on a scale not experienced in most industrialized nations around the world.

A New War Against the Poor

Unfortunately, the economic and political forces that facilitated the reemergence of state lotteries have not abated in the 1990s but have intensified—and lottery sales continue to grow. Although Bill Clinton was elected President on a platform that emphasized a new approach to domestic problems, the modest reforms he proposed were largely stymied by a conservative Congress. When the Republican Party took control of Congress in 1994, Newt Gingrich became Speaker of the House of Representatives and went to work advancing campaign-year promises outlined in the much-publicized "Contract With America." Despite the low level of welfare funding in the United States compared to other industrialized nations, these proposals called for even more austerity for people with low incomes. For example, the Congress— acting largely on myths and misconceptions about people who are poor—cut funds to welfare recipients while making the criteria for welfare eligibility more stringent. Holly Sklar notes:

> The ultimate goal of the Right is to abolish welfare altogether and replace it with nothing—except prisons and, perhaps, poorly funded orphanages. No one should doubt that dismantling welfare—without replacing it with ... progressive initiatives ... will lead to more hunger, homelessness, crime and, as battered women's advocates are warning, the beating and murder of women and children less able to flee their abusers.[13]

Moreover, supporters of the "Contract With America" pushed by the Republican Party in the early 1990s—which critics derisively referred to as the "Contract On America"—cut back on Supplemental Security Income (SSI), a program that assists older people and people who have disabilities, on food stamps and nutrition programs for children and for women who are pregnant or nursing, and on housing assistance, student loans, and employment training. At the same time, these policy-makers shifted even more resources to the rich through new tax benefits and further business deregulation. Many policies and programs on which most people in the United States have come to rely for their health and well-being, such as environmental regulations, health research, and food inspections, were scaled back.[14] Not surprisingly, at the same time the number of people imprisoned in the United States is in the process of doubling in the course of a decade. In 1990 the number of people imprisoned was one million. By 1997 that number reached 1.7 million and was growing.[15]

The federal government's continued championing of the interests of the affluent has been accompanied by the increased concentration of capital. Mega-mergers continue, especially among giant financial institutions, while the rules for the new global economic order created by the powerful and their attendants—NAFTA and the World Trade Organization—bode poorly for the majority of people in the United States and around the world. These trends have most certainly contributed to increases in lottery sales in the United States in the 1990s and will surely contribute to their future growth.

Will contemporary state lotteries eventually fall into public disfavor, like their nineteenth-century predecessors? They are unlikely to succumb to the corruption and fraud that undermined lotteries in the late nineteenth century because, while some abuses and machinations may occur, current safeguards make widespread fraud unlikely. State governments are addicted to lotteries as a source of revenue, and they have too much at stake to permit widespread corruption to occur. One possible threat to the lotteries' continuance, however, is periodic ebbs in lottery sales. Politically conservative and religious critics of lotteries may take advantage of declines in sales to call for the termination of government lotteries.

Such a situation occurred in 1998 in Arizona. The lottery there is dependent on periodic review and reapproval by the legislature, and the lottery was scheduled to end on July 1, 1999. The lottery's managers encountered stagnant sales and an inability to generate interest in new games. (While the lottery netted nearly $259 million in 1996, that amount was less than 1 percent of state revenues.) Political conservatives took advantage of the periodic review and called for the termination of the lottery due to poor sales and what they saw as the effect of lotteries on the work ethic. The Arizona legislature decided to let the public vote on whether the lottery should be extended for another five years. This ostensibly democratic procedure was something of a pretense, however, as state lawmakers knew there was still strong public support for the lottery. Although the U.S. economy was performing well for investors and the affluent in the late 1990s, it was advancing at the expense of the many who continued to look to lotteries to realize their dreams. By a margin of 66.8 percent to 32.2 percent, the citizens voted in November 1998 to continue the lottery until July 1, 2003.

Public support for lotteries has spread even to areas where they once encountered considerable traditional, religious-based resistance, such as Alabama and South Carolina, where lottery creation appears imminent. So, while it is unlikely that lotteries will be repudiated any time soon, gambling-related problems—especially compulsive gambling—have required at least the appearance of government response, even if it is the minimalist, laissez-faire response to social problems in capitalist countries. Interestingly, examples of such government finesse can been seen in both the U.K. and the United States at the national level. The governments' obligatory review of lotteries and other forms of gambling was generated more by organized religion than by the political left.

In the U.K., church leaders of various denominations have continually condemned the lottery as "undermining public culture," and seized on recent lottery-related scandals to call for reform—such as an end to scratch cards and setting maximum jackpots at £1 million. However, when the liberal Labour Party won control of Parliament in 1997 it was in no position to curtail substantially what Stephen Hawking called the "shabby and sleazy" practice. Firmly in the grip of twenty-first-century global capitalist imperatives, including World Trade Organization policies that weaken governments' economic decision-making power, faced with vast inequities in the U.K., and spurred by the existence of lotteries in other European Union nations, the Labour Party could muster only modest reforms. Indeed, reliance on the lottery had become so important, and chances for other sources of public revenues so remote, that one government official called the National Lottery the "greatest opportunity Britain has ever had to regenerate itself."[16] Thus, the Labour Party campaigned on—and enacted when it controlled Parliament in 1998—nominal reforms that were touted as substantive changes that served the public interest. The largely cosmetic endeavor was exemplified by Labour's christening the reformed lottery the "People's Lottery." Reforms included a transfer by 2001 of the lottery's management from the original for-profit consortium with which the government had contracted in 1994 to non-profit management, greater accountability for lottery revenue allocation, new regulation to reduce exploitative and manipulative advertising, and efforts to reduce access by minors to scratch cards and lottery tickets.

Despite its claims of reform, Labour actually increased public reliance on the lottery by adding a new target for lottery funds. Previously, the government's lottery profits were allocated to five "Good Causes": the arts, charities, local sports councils, a Heritage Fund for historical preservation, and a fund for activities to celebrate the new millennium. Labour introduced a sixth "Good Cause," a fund for health, education, and the environment. Critics have pointed out that the five original causes were areas in which government funds were seldom allocated, thus preventing the financial "shell games" that plague lotteries in the United States. However, introducing a fund for health, education, and the environment opened the door for lottery funds to replace existing expenditures. Labour essentially gave the U.K. lottery a face-lift, touting the "Good Causes" it funds and ceremoniously announcing each local project receiving lottery funds. The reforms in reality helped to suppress lottery criticism, fostered additional public support, and, in the end, perpetuated a regressive tax and the trail of social problems it generates.

Similarly, in the United States traditional religious condemnation of gambling and lotteries ostensibly was supported by a conservative, Republican-controlled Congress, which, in 1996, created the National Gambling Impact Study Commission (NGISC) to examine the social implications of gambling. As in the U.K., the U.S. government needed to answer, or to appear to answer, growing questions about problems of gambling addiction, while still largely endorsing the multi-billion-dollar gaming industry.

To its credit, the nine-member Commission took a serious look at the consequences of lotteries and other forms of gambling in the United States. Its June 1999 report supported many of the contentions of anti-gambling groups. The NGISC report particularly rankled state lottery officials by noting that state governments have become "enthusiastic purveyors"[17] of gambling, with lotteries the most widespread form of gambling in the nation. The Commission supported critics' contentions that state lotteries "knowingly target their poorest citizens, employing aggressive and misleading advertising to induce those individuals to gamble away their limited means."[18] The report noted the lotteries' troubling tendencies to promote gambling among young people, their role in the growing problem of compulsive gambling, and the influence of lottery-industry lobbyists over state legislatures.

Nonetheless, the report made no mention of the tumultuous economic and political events of the last quarter century that prompted the emergence of lotteries and other forms of gambling as forms of revenue creation and economic development. In a single, victim-blaming sentence, the report attributed the growth of state lotteries to "stiff public resistance to tax increases as well as incessant demands for increased or improved public services from the same citizens."[19] What is more, the Commission muted its critique by lauding the wonders of gambling as a form of economic development, exemplified by the following statement:

> Sleepy backwaters have become metropolises almost overnight; skyscrapers rise on the beaches at once-fading tourist areas; legions of employees testify to the hope and opportunities that the casinos have brought them and their families; some Indian nations have leapt from prolonged neglect and deprivation to sudden abundance.[20]

The Commission submitted a number of recommendations to the President and Congress for consideration but, as in the U.K., these largely focus on limited efforts to reduce compulsive gambling and ways to provide treatment for gambling addicts. While the Commission asserted that individual states best knew how to regulate themselves, they suggested efforts to reduce exploitative advertising and minors' access to lottery products. So once again, with the support of the state, economic exigencies largely eclipsed moral appeals for fairness and justice.

Notably, criticism from the left, especially about the regressive nature of lotteries, did not figure prominently in the debates in the U.K. and U.S. In the future, it will be particularly important for the Left to articulate its position if true consideration of the public interest is to be brought into discussions about the future of state lotteries, the entire system of unfair taxation, and the vast disparities in the distribution of resources, both in the United States and around the world. As economic distress and insecurity intensify, the people may be more open to the message that their dreams of economic security are most likely to be realized not by a one-in-five-million chance of winning a Lotto (in the U.K. the odds are one in fourteen million), but by the enactment of social policies that address the interests of all individuals. The public needs to understand that only a movement toward economic democracy will bring about a fairer system of taxation, decent wages, health care for all, decent and affordable housing, quality primary and secondary education for every child, and other much-needed changes in the existing system of social arrangements.

One of the left's major challenges is to find ways to question effectively and change a system when the forces of the status quo have, in Miliband's words, "a crushing advantage." And now state lotteries, with their ability to give false hope and inspire dreams of wealth among the disenfranchised and marginalized, buttress the social order and make the struggle for social justice even more difficult.

One advantage for the left, as we have seen, is that people with lower incomes are not as likely to subscribe to system-supporting ideologies as the more affluent. Moreover, history teaches that a widespread acceptance of societal conditions will wax and wane, particularly as economic circumstances change. The left must cultivate effective ways of reaching large numbers of people and must deliver a clear message about the need for, and the benefits of, economic democracy—and it must be prepared to maximize its influence in periods of waning public support for the status quo—in order to spark public support for real change.

It is important that the economic realities and possibilities articulated by the left also include a critique of the system of political representation in the United States. Even if a hard-fought campaign results in the election of a progressive office holder, promotion of a policy that would substantially affect disparities in the distribution of economic resources would receive virtually no support from either major political party. For example, the last U.S. president to promote a progressive tax proposal was Jimmy Carter, in 1977. It was "decimated" by a Congress controlled by Democrats.[21] Likewise, in the 1980s Democratic senator Daniel Patrick Moynihan made a proposal on the floor of the United States Senate that wage earners receive tax cuts and that the regressive federal system of taxation be reversed. In the words of one analyst, "Democratic Senate leaders were struck mute, as though Moynihan had told an obscene joke on the Senate floor."[22] If the state's role as protector of wealth is to be effectively challenged, change in the structure of our system of government will be necessary.

If a political mechanism existed for political influence for low- and moderate-income people, substantial reforms in taxation and other social policies would be more likely to occur. Such mechanisms exist in other nations. Electoral systems in such European countries as the

Netherlands, Switzerland, Germany, and France are organized to provide proportional representation, resulting in any party receiving parliamentary seats in proportion to its share of the total vote. In such systems, labor parties, democratic socialists, environmentalists, and other groups have been successful in promoting more responsible social and economic policies than have been enacted in the United States. This is also why economic disparities are less pronounced in those countries than in the United States. Notably, fairer systems of taxation in other nations fund universal entitlement programs, benefits available to all citizens.[23] Creation of more universal entitlement programs in the United States such as Social Security—would help reduce the victim-blaming and division of society into factions that occur when minimal entitlements are offered only to the very poor. When all citizens receive the same benefits, such as health care, live-able pensions, college tuition, family leave support, quality child care, and the like, they are more likely to recognize their common interests and to resist effectively the self-serving actions of the economically powerful.

Changing to a proportional-representation form of government in the United States, and the power such a change would give to low and moderate-income people, would likely help eliminate many unfair policies, would lead to a fairer system of taxation, and would result in improvement in the quality of life for the vast majority. If state lotteries were not eradicated under such a system, they would at least be played to supplement a respectable standard of living, and not played out of desperation. However, such a possibility has been checked in the United States with its system of winner-take-all representation that has served to maintain the subordination of those whose political inclinations might lead to a restructuring of the economic system. It is unlikely, therefore, that any significant change will take place in the United States unless it is forced by social unrest. In their 1994 book *America: Who Really Pays the Taxes?*, Donald L. Barlett and James B. Steele reflected on their interviews with people across the nation.

> There was a strong sense that the problems, while serious, were not insurmountable..... A question [was] posed over and over again, in one variation or another, by a cross-section of people, from Cherry Hill, New Jersey to Portland, Oregon, from Boston to Miami. The question was asked not by radical students but by a grandmother and a professional person and a blue-collar worker and a white man in a three-piece business suit in Philadelphia, who stated it most bluntly:
>   "Do you really believe these problems can be solved without people taking to the streets?"[24]

History suggests that they are right—that substantive social change, change that truly advances the public interest, rarely occurs without widespread and sustained citizen protest.

Notes

1. Charles A. Beard, *An Economic Interpretation of the Constitution of the United States* (New York: Macmillan, 1941 [1913]), xii.
2. Carl Sagan, *Broca's Brain* (New York: Ballantine Books, 1979), xiii–xiv.
3. Ibid., 104.
4. Charles Horton Cooley, *Social Organization: A Study of the Larger Mind* (New York: Schocken Books, 1962 [1909]), 400.
5. "Study Rates U.S. Low On Helping Poor," *St. Louis Post Dispatch*, September 9, 1991, 1.
6. Ibid., 20.
7. "Gap in Wealth In U.S. Called Widest in West," *New York Times*, April 17, 1995, 1.
8. "The Rich Get Rich Faster," Editorial, *New York Times*, April 18, 1995, A24.
9. Ibid.
10. Harold Kerbo, *Social Stratification and Inequality: Class Conflict in Historical and Comparative Perspective* (New York: McGraw-Hill, 1991), 335.
11. Ibid.
12. Statistic provided by Bruce La Fleur of *La Fleur's Lottery Magazine*, August 23, 1999.
13. Holly Sklar, *Chaos or Community: Seeking Solutions, Not Scapegoats For Bad Economics* (Boston: South End Press, 1995), 101.
14. "Beyond the Contract," *Mother Jones*, March/April 1995, 54–58.
15. Cassandra Burrell, Associated Press, "Nation's Lockups Hold 1.7 Million, Report Says," *Dayton Daily News*, January 19, 1998, 1A.
16. Susannah Herbert, "Puttnam Urges Lottery Rethink," *Electronic Telegraph*, May 1, 1995, 1, http:// www.telegraph.co.uk.
17. National Gambling Impact Study Commission Report (Washington, DC, 1999), 1-4 through 3-5.
18. Ibid., 1-2.
19. Ibid., 1-5.
20. Ibid., 1-1.
21. William Greider, *Who Will Tell the People: The Betrayal of American Democracy* (New York: Touchstone Books, 1992), 89.
22. Ibid., 99.
23. See, for example, the description of the system of universal entitlements in Sweden discussed in Ruth Sidel, *Women and Children Last: The Plight of Poor Women in Affluent America*, Revised Edition (New York: Penguin Books, 1992).
24. Donald L. Barlett and James B. Steele, *America: Who Really Pays the Taxes?* (New York: Touchstone Books, 1994), 344.

INDEX